STORIES AND TOASTS
FOR AFTER DINNER

WITTY
STORIES AND TOASTS

FOR ALL OCCASIONS AND
HOW TO TELL THEM

The Toastmaster, His Duties and Responsibilities. — Toasts and After-Dinner
Stories for all Occasions and
How to Tell Them

BY

NATHANIEL C. FOWLER, Jr.

Author of "How to Save Money," "The Art of Letter-
Writing," "Handbook of Journalism," "The
Art of Story-Writing," etc.

NEW YORK
GEORGE SULLY AND COMPANY

PREFACE

THE author has attempted to present in a concrete and concise way, not only a large number of sensible and appropriate toasts and witty and other after-dinner stories, but also several chapters of general suggestion, which he hopes will be of some value to both the professional and amateur after-dinner speaker and story-teller.

It is obvious that neither the author, nor any one else, could produce more than a limited number of original toasts and after-dinner stories, and it would be inadvisable for him to do so, because, even if he possessed unusual proficiency and ability in this direction, there would be an unavoidable sameness in the result.

The author has, therefore, presented both original and borrowed toasts and after-dinner stories and has not omitted a good toast or story because of its age.

The selected toasts and stories are both new and old, and the author has certainly tried not to present those which are hackneyed or which lack pertinency and point, nor has he given any which cannot be used as a part of an after-dinner address.

As the value of the story depends upon conditions, including environment, as well as upon the quality of the story itself, and as neither conditions nor environment can be anticipated, the author has not classified the stories. Had he done so, he would without doubt have blanketed their effectiveness, because most good stories are applicable to several situations and occasions. To classify them would have been practically impossible, and certainly inadvisable.

CONTENTS

STORIES AND TOASTS
FOR
AFTER DINNER

THE TOASTMASTER

UNLESS the function is entirely informal, and limited to a few diners, all dinners, with post-prandial exercises, are presided over by a man or woman, officially and commonly known as the toastmaster, never toastmistress, the term toastmaster applying to both sexes.

The toastmaster is the presiding officer and directs the exercises. He sits at the centre of the head-table.

If there is a leading or prominent guest, this guest sits at the right of the toastmaster. The guest second in prominence is at his left, the third at the right of the leading guest, the fourth at the left of the second guest, and so on.

After the dinner is over, and the waiters

have cleared the tables, the toastmaster calls the assembly to order, usually by rapping on the table, or on a glass, with a knife, fork, or spoon, and not ordinarily with a gavel.

There is no set rule governing the character of the opening remarks of the toastmaster. Usually his first words are " Please come to order," or " You will come to order," or " Ladies and gentlemen," or " Fellow members," or " Friends," or " Fellow citizens."

It is expected that the opening remarks of the toastmaster will be limited to a few minutes, not exceeding five minutes, although the opening words of some toastmasters last for fifteen minutes, or a half-hour, or even longer; but it is considered in very bad taste to speak for exceeding five minutes, unless the occasion is one of momentous consequence; and, even then, ten minutes would appear to be the limit.

The leading guest or slated speaker, if there be one, may be called upon first or at any time during the exercises.

Many toastmasters prefer to hold the best speaker or the prominent guest until several have preceded him, and may not call upon him until the last; but, generally, the stated speaker, either is the first one to address the assembly, or appears after two or three speakers have preceded him.

There is no set rule, as the order of speaking is optional with the toastmaster.

The toastmaster should be selected with great care. He should either be thoroughly familiar with the subject, if there is one, or intimately acquainted with the speakers and audience, or with all three. If he is a stranger, he is at a great disadvantage.

It is the duty of the toastmaster to introduce each speaker, presumably with appropriate remarks.

The introductory address should seldom exceed five minutes, two or three minutes to be preferred.

If the speaker is to confine himself to a definite subject, the toastmaster should mention it in his introduction; but, if the speaker is " at large," the toastmaster may or may not announce or suggest a subject for him.

It is better for the toastmaster to let the speaker do as he pleases, and not handicap him by announcing a subject.

The toastmaster, in introducing a speaker, should avoid anticipating what the speaker is to say, taking the words out of his mouth, so

to speak. He should not go further than to
announce his subject, with a few appropriate
remarks about him, these remarks, of course,
to be complimentary.

If the toastmaster presents the arguments
of the coming speech, and outlines it in advance, the speaker is at a great disadvantage.

If the speaker is well known to his audience, the toastmaster should avoid any description of his personality, beyond paying
him a well-deserved compliment.

If the speaker is unknown, or is to discourse upon a subject for which he does not
have a reputation, then the toastmaster may
very properly add to his introduction information which will make it easier for the
speaker.

The custom of over-introducing a speaker,
— that is, claiming for him qualities and
abilities which he does not possess, — is not
only in bad taste, but materially handicaps
the speaker.

Many a good speaker has failed because
the toastmaster " billed " him too high, and
claimed for him a proficiency which he did
not possess. The speaker, therefore, was
unable to " deliver the goods." He could
not come up to the expectation of his audi-

ence, and what he said, — good though it
may have been, — was discounted; because
the toastmaster claimed for him what he
could not deliver.

The toastmaster should avoid any display
of learning or education, unless the gatherings be made up of scientists or educators;
but even then simple language is to be preferred.

The principal function of the toastmaster
is to assist the speaker, not to handicap him,
and his introduction should make it easier for
the speaker to proceed, not harder for him.

The introduction should be simple and directly to the point, and should go no further
than to assist in placing both the speaker and
the audience at ease.

There is absolutely no excuse for the toastmaster who attempts to deliver an oration.
It is out of place and in bad taste.

Many post-prandial exercises have been
ruined by foolish toastmasters, who used the
occasions for the display of their ignorance,
egotism, and conceit.

The toastmaster is nothing more or less
than a director. He is there simply to man-
age or direct the affair, to keep the ball rolling, not to be a part of the ball itself. It is

his duty to arrange the speakers in the manner which will be best for them and for their hearers.

If the speeches are informal, and not upon any one subject, the toastmaster should call upon the speakers, alternating the bright with the sober, so that the audience will not be surfeited with any one kind of address.

The toastmaster has a right to limit the time of the speakers, and he may do so in two ways: first, by mentioning in his introductory remarks the time allowed. He can do this in a gentlemanly way, and without offending the speaker, by using such an expression as " I am going to ask the Hon. Mr. Jones to give us five minutes of politics." Or he may be more definite and say " I am going to permit Mr. Jones to talk for five minutes only; not because we don't want him to talk for five hours, but because we have only five minutes at our disposal." Or he may put it in another way. " I wish that we could give Mr. Jones the entire evening, but we can't, because half of the evening has passed and there are six other anxious speakers awaiting their turn, so I am obliged, much against my will, to ask Mr. Jones to consume not less than five, or more than six, minutes."

Secondly, the toastmaster may call a speaker down, if he exceeds the time allowed, or goes beyond reasonable limits. This is an exceedingly difficult thing to do, because the long-winded speaker generally does not possess the sense of proportion and may be offended.

One of the best toastmasters with whom I ever came in contact had a delicate and splendid way of calling a speaker down. I recall an incident. The speaker, who was supposed to occupy not over twenty minutes, had passed his limit. The toastmaster stood up, and, with a smile which would blow sunshine into the darkest cloud, quietly remarked, " Excuse me, my dear sir, but do you know that, if I permit you to talk any longer, I'll lose my job? "

If the speaker exceeds the limit, and it is absolutely necessary for him to be stopped, the toastmaster must do it, whether or not the speaker is offended.

No gentleman can object to this intrusion, because it is not an intrusion, but the exercise of a right.

The toastmaster may be formal if he will. He may interrupt the speaker at any point with some remark like, " Mr. Jones, I deeply regret that I am obliged, on account of the other speakers, to ask you to close your address in two minutes."

Occasionally the speaker, even with this warning, refuses to stop. The toastmaster, certainly, is in a very awkward position. If he does not stop the speaker, he is not faithful to those who appointed him, and is discourteous to the other speakers. At any cost he must call the speaker down, and may say, "Mr. Jones, I am sorry, but I am obliged to demand that you close your speech."

This drastic action is, fortunately, however, seldom necessary.

If there is a printed program, the toastmaster should, as a rule, follow it, but he has the right to transfer the speakers or to give any one preference.

If there is no printed program, the toastmaster is absolute czar, and may do as he pleases, subject to no interference.

Comparatively few men are good toastmasters. Most of them overdo the matter, speak too long, and handicap their speakers by silly or inappropriate introductions. Half of them interfere with the speaker, rather than assist him, and bore the audience.

If you are called upon to preside at a dinner, lean, and lean heavily, toward brevity.

If you are not a good speaker, and cannot handle wit, introduce your speakers in the simplest and shortest way, doing hardly more than calling them by name.

It is far better to use a commonplace expression like, " We will now hear from Mr. Jones," or " Mr. Jones will tell us what he knows about the North Pole," or " Mr. Jones ought to know a lot about Mexico, because he has been there," than to attempt to make a witty, or more appropriate, introduction, when you have not the ability either to prepare it or to speak it.

Many toastmasters rely largely upon the telling of humorous stories, and almost invariably preface their remarks, or end their addresses, with a witty story or recite some humorous incident. This custom is to be encouraged.

A really humorous story pleases every audience, from a scientific convention to a political barbecue. It places the hearers in a receptive mood. It relieves the strain. But never tell a story which is not bright or witty, and, further, one which is not appropriate to the occasion.

The story must either be appropriate to the subject under discussion, or to the audience, or to the speaker called upon. If it is not, it is out of place.

Many toastmasters introduce all of their speakers with a story, and there is no objection to it; in fact, the custom is to be approved, provided the stories are appropriate and are not overdone.

The toastmaster at a serious gathering may tell a few witty or light stories, but he should present them at opportune times, so as to lighten up the address, but not to produce too decided a contrast.

Many toastmasters, not only introduce the speaker, but refer to every speech after it is delivered, summing up to some extent. While this may be done to advantage, I think the custom of saying anything about a speech which has been delivered is usually in bad taste and unfair to the speaker, unless the toastmaster has the faculty of adding to what has been said and of doing it as effectively as has the speaker before him.

Upon general principles, I should advise the toastmaster to confine his remarks to introductions and not to summing-up. If he attempts to sum up, he may make a mess of it, and unintentionally do the speaker an injustice.

The toastmaster should always stand while introducing a speaker, unless the affair be entirely informal, when all of the speakers remain seated. He should remain standing until the speaker has addressed him as " Mr. Toastmaster." He should then bow and be seated.

It is much easier to preside at a gathering at which only one sex is present, than to handle a mixed audience.

The two sexes, however much they may have in common, do not get together as much as they will when civilization passes another milestone. For the present, their interests and tastes are somewhat divided.

It is obvious, therefore, that women are not likely to be intensely interested in what particularly appeals to men, nor will men care, as a rule, for those things which are of peculiar value to women.

It is, therefore, extremely difficult to arrange a function which will be equally interesting, instructive, or entertaining to both sexes.

The toastmaster at a mixed gathering is at a disadvantage. If he is wise, he will confine

his remarks to generalities, rather than to
specific statements, and he will avoid telling
any story which will not be instantaneously
comprehended.

Women, as they run, do not have a developed sense of humor. They do not
appreciate pleasantries which appeal to
men.

Women are not naturally scientific, are un-
familiar with technical terms, and are not
conversant with business methods.

The toastmaster, then, must avoid technical expressions, business terms, and everything else which is not easily understood.

I am not depreciating the quality of the
feminine mind, which, as a matter of fact, is
neither materially nor mentally different
from the masculine; but environment and
conditions have placed woman in a different
sphere from that occupied by man, or, to put
it conversely, man has not been permitted to
enter woman's field. But a difference exists,
and the toastmaster must recognize it, and
he must impress upon himself the undeniable
fact that women will not, as a rule, permit
the frank statements which do not offend
men.

I am not here referring to woman in the

class-room, or the laboratory, but to woman at the banquet or at other public place.

How shall one perfect himself in the art of "toastmastering?" He cannot attain proficiency by book or lesson. To be a good toastmaster, one must have some natural capacity for this work and he needs large experience. This experience he will obtain by actual practice and by intently following other toastmasters.

Observation and practice are the only teachers guaranteed to produce results.

THE TOAST

THE toast, technically speaking, is the presentation, with or without drinking, of a sentiment to which somebody, an individual or an audience, should respond, either by a set or extemporaneous speech, or by rising and silence.

Formerly, the drinking of wine or other liquor accompanied every toast, but to-day probably seventy-five per cent. of toasts are without the cup.

There is no sharp dividing line between a toast and a sentiment, nor is there much difference between responding to a set sentiment and to a special or general subject.

The difference lies largely in the fact that the toastmaster, in introducing one who is to respond, distinctly mentions that he is to speak upon the sentiment, which he, the toastmaster, designates. For example, the toastmaster rises and says, " Here's to the land we live in," " Here's to the flag," " Here's to the ladies," " Here's to our mothers," "Here's to the Grand Army," "Here's to the soldiers," "Here's to science," or to "Art," or "Literature," or "Music," "Here's to the poet."

The expressed toast or sentiment may be short or long, but the shorter the better.

It is perfectly proper to say, "Here's to the ladies," and stop there; but one may lengthen it out, as "Here's to the ladies. Bless them. First in our hearts and first in our pockets."

Another example: "Here's to the flag, the emblem of patriotism, of fraternity, of good will to man; and may the day come when all the flags of civilization, each by itself, each in the glory of its independence, will float from a common staff."

Still another example: "Here's to the Press, civilization's greatest developer, without which nations would be strangers and progress be without the wheels for propulsion."

It is not necessary to begin the toast by "Here's to." These words may be omitted, and the toastmaster may start in by saying, "Music, the voice of the inner soul." Then he may call upon the speaker.

If there is a stated or slated speaker to

respond to the toast, the audience does not
rise; the one called upon immediately stands
up and responds.

If the toast is proposed to some person
present, or to some one who is not present,
the audience rises, whether or not the toast
is drank.

If the person toasted is present, he may
or may not respond, as he pleases. If he
does respond, his remarks should be short
and to the point. If he prefers not to speak,
he may simply bow or say, " I thank you."

Although the presiding officer at a dinner
is known as toastmaster, comparatively few
of the speakers called upon respond to toasts.
They are simply introduced, and speak upon
a designated subject, which may or may not
have been announced on the program or bill
of fare; or they discourse on any subject they
choose. They do not technically respond to
a toast. They are simply speakers. It is,
however, proper for any speaker, whether he
responds to a toast or not, to address the presiding officer as " Mr. Toastmaster."

The responder to a toast should stick to the
subject of his toast. It is not allowable, nor
is it in good taste, to branch off from it. If,
for example, he is called upon to respond to

a toast, say, on "Our Country," his remarks
should be confined entirely to the country,
except that he may incidentally bring other
countries into his speech; and, if he does,
he must do so in the way of comparison, not
allowing any other country to take a prominent part.

If the speaker does not respond to a toast,
but is simply called upon to speak, he may
then address the audience upon any subject,
unless his subject is given him by the presiding officer, in which case he should confine
himself largely to the designated subject,
branching off from it, if he will, but never
putting it one side.

As a rule, after-dinner exercises are likely
to be more entertaining, more instructive,
more amusing, and more satisfactory, if
specific toasts are omitted and the speakers
allowed every liberty.

There is a sort of setness about specified
speeches, which savors of the lecture, and
which is not as acceptable to the average
after-dinner audience as is spontaneity, both
of subject and of speaker.

I should advise, therefore, that, unless the
occasion is a formal one, the speakers be allowed to do about as they please, and that

the toastmaster or presiding officer do no
more than generally specify in his introduction what he would like to have them talk
about. Of course, there must be a certain
amount of regulation and premeditation, if
the occasion is at all formal, or there is a
specific purpose; for example, it is obvious
that, if the dinner is intended to celebrate
some historical event, the speakers for the
most part should discourse upon that event.

If the dinner is to be attended by scientists
wholly, or those interested in one particular
study, the speeches should not greatly depart
from the object which brought the audience
together. But the majority of dinners are
merely social gatherings, where men, or men
and women, meet for good fellowship, to be
entertained, or bored, by those who will,
fortunately or unfortunately, be called upon
to address them. The more liberty given
them, the better is likely to be the result.

THE AFTER - DINNER STORY

THE majority, and, perhaps, a very large majority, of speakers, except lecturers, resort to story-telling, and not a few lectures contain pleasantries and humorous incidents.

Unless the address be upon a very solemn, or extremely serious, subject, the introduction of a story, or the recitation of an incident, humorous or bright, or both, materially adds to the effectiveness of the address, lightens up the dark passages, and makes it more acceptable to any audience.

Probably more than half of the professional speakers begin their addresses by telling a humorous story, or reciting some incident, usually of a light or witty character; and the majority of speakers intersperse their remarks with stories, more or less humorous; and some of them close their addresses with the recitation of a story or incident.

This custom is to be encouraged, but the speaker is cautioned against the over-use of stories, for a superabundance of them de tracts from the argument of the address and makes the teller or speaker ridiculous.

Recently I listened to an address by one of our leading after-dinner talkers. He was a man of liberal education, and had an international reputation as a wit. The subject assigned him was of a serious character, and he handled it in a masterly manner, but he so interspersed his remarks with the recitation of witty and humorous stories that the audience forgot his subject and considered him nothing more or less than a vaudeville artist, a professional story-teller.

He convulsed his audience with laughter, and his stories were received with appreciative applause, but the substance of his remarks was neither heard nor remembered; neither were his stories, for that matter. He was simply a show-man, not an orator or a speaker.

I do not propose to present any rule or regulation for the use of stories.

I should suggest, however, that a humorous story be used at the beginning of a speech, that one or two appear in the body of the speech, and that one be told near the end of it, — provided, always provided, — and I say this most emphatically, — that the stories or the incidents are appropriate to the occasion, that they apply to the subject, or to the environment, or to the audience.

The interjection of stories into a speech, no matter how humorous they may be, is in bad taste, and detracts from the address itself, unless they are appropriate and are told at the opportune time.

Poor wit, which hits the mark, makes a stronger impression than good wit which scatters.

The story which does not help the address by helping the audience has no value and damages the speech.

The professional humorist has a right to tell stories continuously, but the speaker upon a definite subject must use stories only as accessories, not as facts.

After-dinner stories are of two kinds: first, humorous or witty stories, each with a point to it; secondly, serious stories or incidents. Yet the value of the serious story is not independent of brightness; if it is merely serious, without any bright lines for lightening, it may fail of its purpose. Therefore, all after-dinner stories should be bright, whether or not they are humorous, and they must be appropriate.

The after-dinner story should be introduced so as not to appear to be forced into the speech in too abrupt a manner.

The speaker should, as a rule, introduce it in some way like the following: " Speaking of the ocean, I am reminded of a story told me by my friend Captain Jones of the Blue Star Line."

Or, " As I look about me, I recall a similar occasion, when I had the honor to speak before the Rhode Island teachers. In the audience was the oldest school superintendent in America; at least he said he was, and nobody cared to compete with him. After I was through we were thrown together. One of his experiences will well illustrate the point I have just made."

Or, " Ah! I see my old friend Colonel Jones in the audience. As I am a bigger man than he is, — I mean physically, — I am going to tell you what happened to Jones, and how mad Jones was, because what happened to him didn't happen to me instead. The Colonel and I crossed the big pond, etc."

Or, " The last speaker told a mighty good story about what happened to him in Nova Scotia. I have another one which is apropos. When I was in Halifax, last year, etc."

Or, " I can illustrate my point by quoting from an old friend of mine, a Maine farmer. He, like Abraham Lincoln, drove his arguments home by hammering stories into his hearers. Not ten thousand miles away from where we are lived an old chap named Bartholomew, etc."

Or, " I have listened intently, and have deeply appreciated the words of my opponent. He has sincerely and conscientiously attempted to knock the props from under my arguments. He has not succeeded, because their foundations were built upon the solid rocks of truth, and all the storms in Christendom, and all the winds from vocal tornadoes, cannot move them from their established base. May I digress for a moment and liken my opponent to an old chap I used to know, who sawed wood for a living. He was a queer old fellow, and had a logic of his own. One day a log of wood hit him on the head. After the stars had disappeared, he remarked in his drawling voice, etc."

The story may be introduced at the opening of a speech, somewhat as follows: " Mr. Toastmaster, ladies and gentlemen, I cannot, like the last speaker, sail against my own wind. He reminds me very much of a chap

I used to know in Missouri. This fellow
had a long head, a very long head, as thick
as it was long; and he had a way of saying
things without meaning them, etc."

THE QUESTIONABLE STORY AND " DON'TS "

DON'T under any circumstances tell a vulgar, obscene, off-color, or questionable story.

Wit does not need a vulgar setting.

No audience, however low down it may be, has any respect for the speaker who descends to vulgarity or to the obscene, although the members of it may laugh and applaud the off-color story.

The speaker has no right to insult any member of his audience, or to say anything in the way of story-telling, or of pleasantries, which will outrage decency.

I am aware that a large percentage of public speakers, when addressing an audience of men, frequently cross the line of vulgarity, and tell stories which are sure to jar at least a proportion of their hearers.

I am not suggesting that any speaker place himself under the censorship of a Mrs. Grundy, or refuse to use effective slang; nor do I suggest that all of his stories represent ultra-refinement. I am simply protesting against the introduction of anything into a speech which depends upon vulgarity for its effect.

The obscene story-teller has no real respect for himself, and his hearer, although he may vociferously laugh, does not respect the story-teller.

Don't tell a long story. The good story, or, rather, the story which will be appreciated by the audience, is a short one.

There is no room in any speech for a long story. It belongs to the book.

Don't tell a story which will not be understood by every member of the audience.

Don't tell a religious story, which can possibly offend any denomination.

Don't introduce a political story, which will not be acceptable to members of every political party, unless you are delivering a partisan address.

Don't tell a story which will offend any nationality. I do not mean by this that the speaker should avoid witty stories, which, in a pleasant and harmless way, " rap " a country or its people.

Don't tell a story aimed at an insignificant member of an audience. Always fire your stories at some prominent person, who is too big to resent personalities and sarcasm.

Don't tell a story to a popular audience, which depends upon scientific or other special knowledge for its interpretation.

Don't tell a story which is not appropriate, either to the environment, the subject, or to some well-known person.

Don't sarcastically refer to any one, unless you are sure that he will not be sensitive.

When in doubt, don't.

TOASTS

AMERICA and England: May they be cemented by love and affection, cousins of the past and brothers of the present.

A long chord and a short chord to those who make discord.

To America: her lovely women and her brave men.

Americans in unity and unity in Americans.

American virtue: May it always find a protector, but never need one.

America: the nursery of learning, and the birthplace of heroes.

Cork to the heels, cash to the pockets, courage to the hearts, and concord to the heads of all those who stand for America.

Confusion to those who, wearing the mask of patriotism, pull it off and desert the cause of liberty in the hour of trial.

Confusion to all those who attempt to disunite the interests of our country.

Community, unity, navigation, and trade.

Confusion to those despots who combine against the liberties of mankind.

Fill to the brim, and let the goblet's face
Smile with the sparkling purple — Drink,
My friends, the health —
        " Our Country ! "
Ever may she prove the rock of liberty,
And her brave sons, to distant ages,
Emulate your zeal.

Here's a health unto our President,
Confusion to our enemies,
And he that will not pledge his health,
I wish him neither wit nor wealth,
Nor yet a rope to hang himself.

Long live the men who seek their people's love.

May every future President of the United States be as patriotic as our President.

May we never know any difference between our country and others, save the oceans which separate them.

May the skin of our foes be turned into parchment, and our rights written thereon.

May the sword of Justice be swayed by the hand of Mercy.

May the seeds of dissension never find growth in the soil of America.

May those who root up the Tree of Liberty be crushed by its fall.

May our counsels be wise, and our commerce increase,
And may we ever experience the blessings of peace.

May the Tree of Liberty flourish around the globe, and every human being partake of its fruit.

May all mankind make free to enjoy the blessings of liberty, but never take the liberty to subvert the principles of freedom.

> May corruption be chained,
> And truth maintained.

May wealth and commerce ne'er desert our shore,
Till hoary-headed Time himself shall be no more.

May true patriotism ever guard the public weal, and extinguish the torch of discord.

May the weight of our taxes never bend the back of our credit.

May the Sons of Liberty marry the Daughters of Virtue.

May our trade and manufactures be unrestrained by the fetters of monopoly.

May every civil government be founded on the natural rights of man.

May all civil distinctions among men be founded upon public utility.

May America, like a tennis ball, rebound the harder she is struck.

May the glory of America never cease to shine.

Prosperity: may it ever be the rising sun of America.

Religion without priest-craft, and politics without party.

May the tar who loses one eye in the defense of his country never see distress with the other.

Short shoes and long corns to the enemies of progress.

In the voyage of life may Content be our fellow passenger.

May the Boat of Pleasure always be steered by Pilot Wisdom.

May those who escape the quicksands of jealousy never run on the shoals of indifference.

May gales of prosperity steer us into the Port of Happiness.

May the pilot of reason guide us to the Harbor of Rest.

May rudders govern, and ships obey.

May no son of the ocean be devoured by his mother.

May the mainbrace ever be well spliced.

May light breezes waft us safely but not rapidly to the haven of future felicity.

The Constitution of the United States: may it flourish to the latest posterity, and may the merchants of our country never traffic in blood.

May the Barque of Friendship never founder on the Rock of Deceit.

The seed: and may it always bring a springtide of joy.

The wind that blows, the ship that goes, and the lass that loves a sailor.

The tar that sticks like pitch to his duty.

Love in every breast, liberty in every heart, and learning in every head.

Love to one, friendship to a few, and goodwill to all.

May Love and Reason be friends, and Beauty and Prudence marry.

May the sparks of love brighten into a flame.

May we kiss whom we please and please whom we kiss.

May we never overleap the bounds of prudence, or trespass on the bosom of friendship.

The Press: the great correcter of abuses, the shield of the oppressed, and the terror of the oppressor.

May the bud of affection be ripened by the sunshine of sincerity.

May every woman have a protector, but not a tyrant.

May those who love truly be always believed; And those who deceive us be always deceived.

The Press: the great bulwark of our liberties; and may it ever remain unshackled.

The Light of Civilization is fed by printer's ink.

May Poverty always be a day's march behind us.

May our great men be good, and our good men be great.

May Good Nature and Good Sense get married.

May our afflictions throw our virtues into practice.

May we be happy, and our enemies know it.

May our faults be written on the seashore, and every good action prove a wave to wash them out.

May the polished heart make amends for the rough countenance.

May every smooth face proclaim a smoother heart.

May the rough road of adversity lead us to final prosperity.

May the shackles of prejudice never fetter the mind.

May the best day we have seen be the worst we have to come.

May we never envy those who are happy, but strive to imitate them.

May the faults of our neighbors be dim, and their virtues glaring.

May the rich be charitable, and the poor be grateful.

May artificial coloring be always perceived through every veil of disguise.

May honesty never be ashamed of an unfashionable garment.

The musician's toast: May the lovers of harmony never be in want of a note, and their enemies be hanged by a common chord.

The three A's: Abundance, Abstinence, and Annihilation; Abundance to the poor, Abstinence to the intemperate, Annihilation to the wicked.

The three F's: Friendship, Feeling, and Fidelity; Friendship without interest, Feeling for the depressed, Fidelity to truth.

The three Generals in Peace: General Peace, General Plenty, General Satisfaction.

The three Generals in Power: General Employment, General Industry, General Comfort.

The three H's: Health, Honor, and Happiness; Health to all the world, Honor to those who seek for it, Happiness in our homes.

The three L's: Love, Life, and Liberty; Love pure, Life long, Liberty boundless.

The three L's: Love, Loyalty, and Length of Days.

The three M's: Modesty, Moderation, and Mutuality; Modesty in our discourse, Moderation in our wishes, Mutuality in our affection.

The three M's: Mirth, Music, and Moderation; Mirth at every board, Music in all instruments, Moderation in our desires.

The four comforts of life: Love, Liberty, Health, and a Contented Mind.

May the wings of love never lose a feather.

The surgeon's toast: The man who bleeds for his fellow men.

The glazier's toast: He who takes pains to see his way through life.

The market man's toast: May he spring up like vegetables, have a turnip nose, a radish cheek, and carrotty hair, and may his heart be as soft as a cabbage and never rotten at the core.

The carpenter's toast: May he be well glued who gets a-board wrongfully.

The tailor's toast: May he always cut bad company.

The baker's toast: May he never be crusty.

The printer's toast: May his wife never lock him up.

Fair days, fair times, and fair ladies.

Gratitude to preserve our old friends, and good behavior to procure new ones.

Health of body, peace of mind, an extra shirt, and a dollar.

May we look forward with pleasure, and backward without regret.

May we never break a joke to crack a reputation.

May we always sail in pleasure's boat.

May no lazy man ever have a careless master.

May every man be wise enough to take that counsel which even a fool can give.

May we always have more occasion for the cook than for the doctor.

May our injuries be written in sand and our friendships in marble.

May we strengthen the weak, give light to
    the blind,
Clothe the naked, and be friends to mankind.

May Justice and Truth on the forecastle
    stand,
And Religion dictate the word of command.

May we never want for bait when we fish for content.

May the bud of sincerity ever blossom in the bosom of friendship.

May we live respected and die regretted.

May we never mask, save at a masquerade.

May we never murmur without a cause, or ever have cause to murmur.

May we be slaves to nothing but our duty, and friends to nothing but merit.

May the good tool always have a good workman.

The girl that is witty,
The girl that is pretty,
The girl with an eye as black as a sloe;
Here's to girls of each station
Throughout the whole nation,
And, in particular, the one that I know.

May the bark of friendship never founder in the well of deception.

May we be richer in friends than in money.

May old friends never be forgot for new ones.

A health to all those whom we love,
A health to all those who love us,
A health to all those who love them that love
    those
Who love those that love them who love us.

May difference of opinion never alter
friendship.

Gratitude to our friends and grace to our
foes.

May the hinges of friendship never rust.

A friend who is true — the sunshine of
life.

All absent friends on land and sea.

May we always have a friend and know his
value.

May the end of the chase be the beginning
of happiness.

May those who love the crack of the whip
never want a brush to follow.

The sportsman that never beats about the
bush.

The man that catches fair game and
doesn't poach on another's preserves.

Rod and line: may they never part company.

The gallant hound that never goes on a false scent.

Bat and ball. Long may they be honestly opposed in the field.

Our " Masters:" may they always show us good game, and deal well with their packs.

May the sweet savor of our good deeds lie well when we have " gone over the last fence."

Education — The only interest worthy the deep, controlling anxiety of the thoughtful man.

Woman — Gentle, patient, self-denying; without her man would be a savage; and the earth a desert.

Our Firesides — Our heads may not be sharpened at colleges, but our hearts are graduates of the hearths.

Our Noble Selves — Why not toast ourselves, and praise ourselves; since we have the best means of knowing all the good in ourselves.

Woman — A Mistress of Arts, who robs a bachelor of his degree, and forces him to study philosophy by means of curtain lectures.

The Judiciary — As sword-bearers to justice, we respect her administrators. Though they often base their decisions on common law, theirs are no common minds.

May your friends be as true to you as you are to them.

May foreign fashions never corrupt American manners.

May the fiery trials of adversity lead us to scenes of bliss.

May our pleasures be boundless while we have time to enjoy them.

Here's to the health of everybody, lest somebody should feel himself slighted.

May we always be under the orders of General Peace, General Plenty and General Prosperity.

May we never feel want, or want feeling.

May we never know sorrow but by name.

Health, happiness, riches and a good wife.

May we always be in possession of the power to please.

May our wants be reduced and our comforts increased.

May he who turns his back on a friend fall into the hands of his enemies.

May we look upon the faults of others with the same eye we look upon our own.

May we all travel to one destination — happiness; although we may go by different roads.

May we have the wit to discover what is true and the fortitude to practice what is good.

Here's to you and me and all of us, and to all who, whether they know us or not, have the divine spark of good-fellowship glowing in their hearts.

May the sons of America never forget the struggles of their fathers and the fortitude of their mothers.

May Americans share the sweets of liberty and ever contend for the freedom and happiness of the human race.

" Breathes there a man with soul so dead,
Who never to himself has said,
    This is my own, my native land;
Whose heart has ne'er within him burned,
As home his footsteps he hath turned
    From wandering on a foreign strand? "

May the stars and the eagle standard be
ever crowned with the laurel of victory.

May the stars of America ever light up the
ocean, and her sails whiten every sea.

May those who, discontented with their
own country, seek a home in foreign parts,
never find one like America.

May the ships of America ever bear bright
sails, good news, good cargoes, and good
hearts, and have fair winds and light seas.

Memory — May it always be a store-
house, not a lumber room.

Home — A world of strife shut out, and
a world of love within.

Charity — A physician whose sole fee is
the consciousness of doing good.

Our friends — May the present have no
burdens for them and futurity no terrors.

The Trade of America — The Workshop of the World: Let its prosperity become as unbounded as its resources and industry are unlimited.

The fee simple and the simple fee,
    And all the fees entail,
Are nothing when compared with thee,
    Thou best of fees — female.

Everybody takes pleasure in returning small obligations; many go so far as to acknowledge moderate ones; but there is hardly any one who does not repay great obligations with ingratitude.

Here's to you, old friend, may you live a
    thousand years,
Just to sort of cheer things in this vale of
    human tears;
And may I live a thousand too — a thousand
    — less a day,
'Cause I wouldn't care to be on earth and
    hear you'd passed away.

Here's to the bride and mother-in-law,
Here's to the groom and father-in-law,
Here's to the sister and brother-in-law,
Here's to the friends and friends-in-law,
May none of them need an attorney-at-law.

The wimmin!
So let us all; yes, by that love
  Which all our lives rejoices,
By those dear eyes that speak to us
  With love's seraphic voices.
By those dear arms that will infold us
  When we sleep forever,
By those dear lips that kiss the lips
  That may give answer never,
By mem'ries lurkin' in our hearts
  An' all our eyes bedimmin',
We'll drink a health to those we love
  An' who love us — the wimmin!

Here's to matrimony — the high sea for
which no compass has yet been invented!

Money talks but nobody notices what kind
of grammar it uses.

Here's to those who love us,
  And here's to those who don't,
A smile for those who are willing to,
  And a tear for those who won't.

Here's to the Bachelor, so lonely and gay,
For it's not his fault he was born that way.
And here's to the Spinster, so lonely and good,
For it's not her fault — she hath done what
  she could.

Two ears and but a single tongue
By nature's laws to man belong.
The lesson she would teach is clear,
Repeat but half of what you hear.

Here's to the prettiest,
Here's to the wittiest,
Here's to the truest of all who are true.
Here's to the neatest one,
Here's to the sweetest one,
Here's to them all in one — here's to you.

Woman needs no introduction; she speaks for herself.

May the thorns of life only serve to give longer life to its flowers.

Here's to the Press, the School, and the Petticoat, — the three ruling powers of the day. The first spreads knowledge, the second teaches it, and the third spreads considerably.

May opinions never float in the sea of ignorance.

May the sunshine of comfort dispel the clouds of despair.

May the devil cut the toes of all our foes,
That we may know them by their limping.

Uneasy looks the face that wears a frown.

May the pleasures of youth bring us con-
solation in old age.

Liberty all over the world, and everywhere
else.

May every patriot love his native country,
whether he was born in it or not.

May friendship be the seed of kindness,
and passion the sun which ripens it into love.

Here's to the maiden of bashful fifteen;
　　Here's to the widow of fifty;
Here's to the flaunting, extravagant queen;
　　And here's to the housewife that's thrifty!
　　　　Let the toast pass;
　　　　Here's to the lass;
I'll warrant she'll prove an excuse for the
　　glass.

Saint Patrick was a gentleman,
　　Who, through strategy and stealth,
Drove all the snakes from Ireland —
　　Here's a bumper to his health.
But not too many bumpers,
　　Lest we lose ourselves, and then
Forget the good Saint Patrick,
　　And see the snakes again.

The man of experience knows better: —
    O! the neatness of their neatness when
       they're neat,
    O! the fleetness of their fleetness when
       they're fleet,
        But the neatness of their neatness
        And the fleetness of their fleetness
    Is as nothing to the sweetness when they're
       sweet.

There are girls whom we fool with
And girls whom we're cool with
    And girls whom we spoon with for fun,
There are girls whom we kiss
And there're girls whom we'd miss,
    But we never can love more than one.

A freehold in happy land, untaxed and un-mortgaged.

Virtue for a guide, fortune for an attendant.

May we never condemn that in a brother which we would pardon in ourselves.

May hope be the physician when calamity is the disease.

May we never find danger lurking on the borders of security.

Here's to the happiest days of my life
That I spent in the arms of another man's
wife; —
My mother, God bless her!

May we always look forward to better things, but never be discontented with the present.

May we be roused, but not rendered desperate by calamity.

Beauty is only skin deep. But it takes some time to get through the preliminary enamel.

May the sunshine of plenty dispel the clouds of care.

The good die young —
Here's hoping you live to a ripe old age.

And what if court or castle vaunt
  Its children loftier born? —
Who heeds the silken tassel's flaunt
  Beside the golden corn?
They ask not for the dainty toil
  Of ribboned knights and earls,
The daughters of the virgin soil,
  Are freeborn Yankee girls.

Holmes.

A fig then for Burgundy, Claret or Mountain,
　A few scanty glasses must limit your wish.
But here's to the toper that goes to the foun-
　　tain,
　The drinker that verily " drinks like a
　　fish."

Thomas Hood.

Here's to the press, the pulpit and the petti·
　　coat.
The three ruling powers of the day:
The first spreads knowledge,
The second spreads morals,
And the third spreads over a multitude of
　　sins.

　　A welcome then to joy and mirth,
　　　From hearts as fresh as ours,
　　To scatter o'er the dust of earth,
　　　Their sweetly mingled flowers.

Here's to the wings of love;
May they never moult a feather,
Until your little barque and my little barque
Sail down the stream together.

　　Here's to the girl who's bound to win
　　　Her share at least of blisses,
　　Who knows enough not to go in,
　　　When it is raining kisses.

Judged by no o'erzealous vigor,
    Much this mystic throng expresses:
Bacchus was the type of vigor,
    Silenus of excesses.

Longfellow.

Oh Woman! Lovely Woman!
You're just like a gun;
You're loaded up with powder
And wadded most a ton;
You set your cap with care,
And with a " bang " you slyly shoot
Your eyeballs at his stare.
OH FUDGE!

Here's to those who'd love us
    If we only cared.
Here's to those we'd love,
    If we only dared.

I would advise a young man to pause
    Before he takes a wife;
In fact I see no earthly cause
    Why he should not pause for life.

Let schoolmasters puzzle their brain
    With grammar and nonsense and learning;
Good liquor, I stoutly maintain,
    Gives genius a better discerning.

Goldsmith.

Food fills the wain, an' keeps us livin';
Tho' life's a gift no worth receivin'
When heavy dragged in pine and grievin';
     But oil'd by thee,
The wheels o' life gae down-hill, scrievin',
    Wi' rattlin' glee.

Burns.

No North, no South, no East, no West, no
    one can say who loves it best;
Each loyal heart it thrills to see this Emblem
    of the Free.
Those stripes of red, that field of blue, those
    stars that sparkle like the dew,
Our joy and pride shall ever be, this flag of
    liberty.

      May we live to learn well,
      And learn to live well.

O wad some pow'r the giftie gie us,
To see oursels as others see us!
It wad frae mony a blunder free us.

Burns.

Were't the last drop in the well,
    As I gasp'd upon the brink,
Ere my fainting spirit fell,
    'Tis to thee that I would drink.

Byron.

Here's to health to those we love best —
Our noble selves — God bless us;
None better and many a damn sight worse.
Drink to-day, and drown all sorrow;
You shall, perhaps, not do it to-morrow.
            Beaumont and Fletcher.

Long Life to the Grape! for when summer
    has flown,
The age of our nectar shall gladden our own:
We must die — who shall not? — may our
    sins be forgiven,
And Hebe shall never be idle in Heaven.
            Byron.

On thee, in whom at once conspire
    All charms which heedless hearts can move,
Whom but to see is to admire,
    And Oh! forgive the word — to love.
            Byron.

The world is filled with flowers,
    The flowers are filled with dew,
The dew is filled with love
    And you and you and you.

Here's to the friends we class as old,
    And here's to those who are new;
May the new grow to us old,
    And the old ne'er grow to us new.

Kisses warm, kisses cold,
Kisses timid, kisses bold,
Kisses joyful, kisses sad,
Kisses good, kisses bad,
Here's to kisses new and old,
Pass the bowl ere I go mad.

Abby Drummond.

Here's to the chaperone:
    May she learn from Cupid,
Just enough blindness
    To be sweetly stupid.

Let's be gay, right while we may,
    And seize all love with laughter,
I'll be true as long as you
    And not a moment after.

Again, thou best beloved, adieu!
    Ah! if thou couldst o'ercome regret;
Nor let thy mind past joys review —
    Our only hope is to forget.

Byron.

Here's to woman, whose heart and whose soul
    Are the light and the life of each spell we
        pursue;
Whether sunn'd at the tropics or chilled at
        the pole,
    If woman be there, there is happiness, too.

Here's to you two and to we too;
  If you two love we two,
  As we two love you two,
  Then here's to we four:
But if you two don't love we two
  As we two love you two
Then here's to we two
  And no more.

Health to the bold and dashing coquette,
  Who careth not for me;
Whose heart, untouched by love as yet,
  Is wild and fancy free.

    Laugh at all things,
      Great and small things,
  Sick or well, at sea or shore;
      While we're quaffing,
      Let's have laughing,
  Who the devil cares for more?
                            Byron.

Here's to Love, a thing so divine;
  Description makes it but the less.
'Tis what we feel but cannot define,
  'Tis what we know but cannot express.

A good horse, a warm house, a snug estate,
and a pretty wife, to every one who deserves
them.

Laugh, and the world laughs with you;
  Weep, and you weep alone,
For the sad old earth must borrow its mirth,
  But has trouble enough of its own.
Sing, and the hills will answer;
  Sigh, it is lost on the air,
The echoes bound to a joyful sound,
  But shrink from voicing care.

Rejoice, and men will seek you;
  Grieve, and they turn and go.
They want full measure of all your pleasure,
  But they do not need your woe.
Be glad, and your friends are many;
  Be sad, and you lose them all, —
There are none to decline your nectar'd wine
  But alone you must drink life's gall.

Feast, and your halls are crowded;
  Fast, and the world goes by.
Succeed and give, and it helps you to live,
  But no man can help you die.
There is room in the halls of pleasure
  For a large and lordly train,
But one by one we must all file on
  Through the narrow aisles of pain.
                    Ella Wheeler Wilcox.

Knock, and the world knocks with you,
  Boast, and you boast alone.
The bad old earth is a foe to mirth,
  And has a hammer as large as your own.
Buy, and the gang will answer,
  Sponge, and they stand and sneer;
The revelers join in a joyous sound
  And shout while drinking beer.

Be rich, and the men will seek you,
  Poor, and they turn and go —
You're a mighty good fellow when you are
    mellow,
  And your pockets are lined with dough.
Be flush, and your friends are many,
  Go broke, and you lose them all.
You're a dandy old sport at $4.00 a quart,
  But not if you chance to fall.

Praise, and the cheers are many,
  Weep, and the world goes by,
Be smooth and slick and the gang will stick
  As close as a hungry fly.
There is always a crowd to help you
  A copious draught to drain,
When the gang is gone you must bear alone
  The harrowing stroke of pain.

A little health, a little wealth,
    A little house and freedom,
With some few friends for certain ends,
    But little cause to need 'em.

And the night shall be filled with music,
    And the cares that infest the day
Shall fold their tents like the Arabs,
    And as silently steal away.
                                        Longfellow.

I will drink to the woman who wrought my
      woe
In the diamond morning of long ago;
To the splendor caught from the orient skies
That thrilled in the dark of her hazel eyes,
Her large eyes filled with the fire of the south,
And the dewy wine of her warm red mouth.
                                        Winter.

May every worthy brother, who is willing
to work and labor through the day, be happy
at night, with his friend, his love, and a cheerful home.

And fill them high with generous juice,
    As generous as your mind;
And pledge me in the generous toast —
    " The whole of human kind ! "
                                        Burns.

May we be happy when alone and cheerful when in company.

May we never desire what we cannot obtain.

May we learn to be frugal before we are obliged to be so.

Then fill a fair and honest cup, and bear it
        straight to me,
The goblet hallows all it holds, whate'er it be;
And may the cherubs on its face, protect me
        from the sin,
That dooms one to those dreadful words, —
    " My dear, where have you been? "

                                Holmes.

There is nothing on earth he will not devour,
From a tutor in seed to a freshman in flower;
No sage is too gray, no youth is too green,
And you can't be too plump, though you're
        never too lean.

                                Holmes.

AFTER - DINNER STORIES

IF the other speakers read their manu-
scripts, or it appears that most of the speeches
are committed to memory, or have been prepared with great care, you may, if you speak
extemporaneously, begin with a remark like
" I would rather be an extemporaneous fool
than a premeditated ass."

An introductory remark like this assures an
audience that you are not more than partially
prepared, and is a confession which will be
appreciated, even though you may deliver a
well connected address.

If the attendance is unexpectedly small, due
to stormy weather, or to other unavoidable
condition, you may begin, after addressing
the presiding officer, somewhat as follows:
" Ladies and Gentlemen, I am very much
disappointed at the smallness of my audience,
and yet I cannot say that I blame those who
were fortunate enough to remain away. As

I came into the hall with your president, I turned to him and said, ' Mr. Jones, don't you ever have a larger gathering than this? ' and he replied quietly, ' Oh, yes, when we have a real attraction ! ' "

Occasionally it is not in bad taste to belittle yourself, or to present humorously the impression that nobody wants to hear you, and that you are out of place.

The following story well illustrates it, and may be introduced somewhat as follows :

Something 'way inside of me, — it may be the unexpected pricking of my alleged conscience, — tells me that I am not unlike a fellow who used to live in a town not a thousand miles from where we are. There was a fashionable ball in progress, and he, undressed for it, and unfit to attend it, forced his way between the guardians at the door. At a signal from the floor manager, two burly policemen threw him out into the hall.

Undaunted, he returned, and the officers threw him down one flight of stairs. He picked himself up, and entered the ball room again. He was then thrown down two flights of stairs; but this seemed to have no

effect upon him mentally, although it may
have touched him physically. He bounded
back again, and then was thrown down two
flights of stairs, and kicked into the street.
He picked himself up, cast off the daze, and
remarked to a passing friend, " Say, Bill, do
you know that something tells me, and some-
how I feel, that them fellows up there didn't
want me."

You can then proceed with your speech,
perhaps prefacing it with the further remark
that you will keep on talking until you are
thrown out, or that you will stop before the
throwing-out time.

Dean Swift said that it required a surgical
operation upon a Scotchman to make him see
the point of a joke. No doubt the celebrated
wit referred to an English joke. A young
Englishman at a party mostly composed of
Scotchmen made several attempts to crack a
joke, and, failing to evoke a smile from his
companions, he became angry, and exclaimed,
" Why, it would take a gimlet to put a joke
into the heads of you Scotchmen! "

One of them replied, " Ay; but the gimlet
wud need tae be mair pointed than thae
jokes."

The late Chief Justice Waite, a man of extreme dignity, started for Baltimore one afternoon many years ago from the old Baltimore & Ohio station. He discovered, to his horror, that he had only a few pennies in his pockets. His train was due to depart in a few minutes, and his engagement was an important one. He looked round for a friend; but found none. So he filed boldly up in line to the ticket office. When he reached the window, he smiled pleasantly at the agent and asked him if he recognized him.

" Naw, I don't! " snarled that amiable official. " What do you want? "

" I want a ticket to Baltimore and return," replied the Justice. " I am Chief Justice of the Supreme Court. I have no money with me. I must have forgotten my purse. I can give you my personal check — "

" Oh, you can, can you? " interrupted the agent wrathfully. " You mean — you can't! That game don't go with me. I just had two members of the Cabinet try to work me for tickets, and the Supreme Court gag don't go half as good! Brush by! There's others behind you with the price! "

Justice Waite was dumbfounded. He

couldn't fine the young man for contempt of court; so he just glared at him and blushed and perspired.

He dashed out of the station in hope of meeting some one who could identify him. He had only a minute or two left. At the entrance of a saloon across the street he accosted the proprietor, a short haired, freckled faced, long and lank Irishman, with the frantic inquiry:

" Do you know me? "

" Sure I do, yer Honor," said the man behind the bar. " Ye are wan of the bosses of the Supreme Coort. I see ye ivery day goin' by here on the cars."

" Will you cash a check for me? Quick! I have no time to explain! " And the excited Justice grabbed a pen from the desk near by and began to write like mad.

" Sure I will," agreed the Irishman promptly. " I have seen ould b'ys off on a tear befure git out of money. Trust me, Sor, I'll say nothin'. Is it a twinty ye want? Here ye are. Will ye have a dhrink befure ye go? "

But the Chief Justice was on his way across the street, and he just managed to catch his train.

There were no vacant seats in the car, but as a comely looking woman entered an elderly man near the door attempted to rise, but she at once forced him back into his seat. "Thank you," she said, "but please don't do that. I am perfectly able to stand."

"But, madam, allow — "

"I insist upon your keeping your seat," interrupted the woman, with her hands on his shoulders. The man continued his efforts to rise, saying: "Madam, will you kindly permit me to — "

With another push the woman again forced him back, insisting that she couldn't think of accepting his seat.

With one supreme effort the man forced her aside. "Madam," he exclaimed, "you have already carried me three blocks beyond my destination. I don't care whether you take my seat or not, but I wish to leave this car."

"Shall I have your lunch brought up to you on deck here, dear?" asked the husband of the seasick wife.

"No, love; have it thrown straight overboard; it will save time — and trouble."

A story is told of two Irish farmers who had not seen each other for a long time, and who met at a fair. They had a lot of things to tell each other.

" Shure, it's married Oi am," said Murphy.

" You don't tell me so," said Moran.

" Fai' yes," said Murphy, " and Oi've got a foine, healthy boy, which the neighbors say is the very pictur' o' me."

Moran looked for a moment at Murphy, who was not remarkable for his good looks, and then said:

" Ah, well, what's the harm as long as the child's healthy? "

Mark Twain once asked a neighbor if he might borrow a set of his books. The neighbor replied ungraciously that he was welcome to read them in his library, but he had a rule never to let his books leave his house. Some weeks later the same neighbor sent over to ask for the loan of Mark Twain's lawnmower.

" Certainly," said Mark, " but since I make it a rule never to let it leave my lawn you will be obliged to use it there."

I am rejoiced. The pleasure that follows disappointment is the height of enjoyment. When I came here to-night, I was afraid that I should not be called upon, and my feelings, I think, were something like those of the man who had prepared himself to be hanged, and then suffered mortal anguish because he was reprieved.

Two men were hotly discussing the merits of a book. Finally one of them, himself an author, said to the other.

"No, John, you can't appreciate it. You never wrote a book yourself."

"No," retorted John, "and I never laid an egg, but I'm a better judge of an omelet than any hen in the State."

"Well," said the doctor cheerfully, "how do you feel this morning? Any aches or pains?"

"Yes," answered the patient, "it hurts me to breathe; but the only trouble now seems to be with my breath."

"Oh," said the physician, still more cheerfully, "I'll give you something that will soon stop that."

The mistress of the house had been to a concert, and when she returned she was met by the servant with: " Baby was very ill while you were out, mum."

" Oh, dear!" said Mrs. Youngwife. " Is he better?"

" Oh, yes, mum; he's all right now, but he was bad at first. I found his medicine in the cupboard."

" Good gracious! What have you given the child? There's no medicine in the cupboard."

" Oh, yes, there is; it's written on it." And then the girl triumphantly produced a bottle labeled " Kid Reviver."

A Scotch minister was walking through a street in the village one misty evening when he fell into a deep hole. There was no ladder by which he could make his escape and he began to shout for help. A passing laborer heard his cries, and, looking down, asked who he was. The minister told him, whereupon the laborer remarked:

" Weel, weel, ye needna kick up sic a noise. You'll no be needed afore Sawbath, an' this is only Wednesday nicht."

One hostess, who lacked tact, at dinner placed a learned and somewhat deaf college professor beside a débutante. The girl found the professor very unresponsive, but finally she noticed a dish of fruit, and in desperation asked if he liked bananas.

After being asked several times to repeat the question, her voice being raised each time, attracting the attention of the whole table, she was horrified when the learned man riveted her with a disapproving look, and remarked very distinctly: " My dear young woman, I had hoped that I had misunderstood your question; but, since you persist, I must say that I prefer the old-fashioned nightshirt."

" Now," said the lawyer in court, " William, look at the Judge and tell him who made you? "

William, who was considered pretty stupid, screwed up his face, looked thoughtful, and somewhat bewildered, replied: " Moses."

" That will do," said the lawyer, addressing the Court. " The witness says he supposes Moses made him. That is not an intelligent answer, and I submit that it is not sufficient for him to be sworn as a witness capable of giving evidence."

" Mr. Judge," said William, " may I ax the lawyer a question?"

" Certainly," said the Judge.

" Well, then, Mr. Lawyer, who d'ye s'pose made you?"

" Aaron," said the lawyer, imitating the witness.

After the mirth had somewhat subsided the witness drawled out: " Wall, Judge, now we do read in the Book that Aaron once made a calf, but who'd thought the darned critter had got in here?"

" Children," said the teacher, instructing the class in composition, " you should not attempt any flights of fancy; simply be yourselves and write what is in you. Do not imitate any other person's writings nor draw inspiration from outside sources."

As a result of this advice one bright lad turned in the following: " We should not attempt any flights of fancy, but write what is in us. In me there is my stommick, lungs, hart, liver, two apples, one piece of pie, one stick of lemon candy and my dinner."

President and Mrs. Hadley were on a train bound for New York, where Yale's President was to speak before a national convention. He made use of the hour and twenty minutes he spent in the train by rehearsing his speech in a low voice, using his hands to emphasize certain passages.

A kindly matron who was sitting directly behind Mr. and Mrs. Hadley, and who had been watching and listening, leaned forward, and, tapping Mrs. Hadley on the shoulder, said feelingly: " You have my sincere sympathy, my poor woman; I have one just like him at home."

During a lecture a well-known authority on economics mentioned the fact that in some parts the number of men was larger than that of women, and he added humorously:

" I can therefore recommend the ladies to emigrate to that part of the world."

A young lady seated in one of the last rows got up, and, full of indignation, was leaving the room rather noisily, whereupon the lecturer remarked:

" I did not mean that it need be done in such a hurry as that."

When Mark Twain was living in Hartford, Connecticut, where Dr. Doane, now Bishop of Albany, was rector of an Episcopal church, he went to hear one of the clergyman's best sermons. After it was over Mark approached the Doctor and said politely:

"I have enjoyed your sermon this morning. I welcomed it as I would an old friend. I have a book at home in my library that contains every word of it."

"Why, that can't be, Mr. Clemens," replied the rector.

"All the same, it is so," said Twain.

"Well, I certainly should like to see that book," rejoined the rector with dignity.

"All right," replied Mark; "you shall have it," and the next morning Doctor Doane received with Mark Twain's compliments a dictionary.

Robert was home from college for the Christmas holidays and had just left his father and a neighbor.

"Your son," said the neighbor, "is pursuing his studies at college, isn't he?"

"I guess so," said the father; "he's always behind."

A young lady called one day on Rubinstein, the great pianist, who had consented to listen to her playing.

"What do you think I should do now?" she asked, when she had finished.

"Get married," was Rubinstein's answer.

"Norah," said her mistress severely, "if you have that policeman in the kitchen again I shall speak to him."

"Go as far as ye like, Mum," said Norah, "but yez'll niver git him. We're to be married next Chuesday."

The new Senator from Kentucky is a great fisherman and enjoys nothing more than to relate some tale of the amateur.

On one occasion in Kentucky there was observed a man who had never fished before. His rod was new and shiny. He was whipping a trout stream, when, by some chance, he got a bite. He did not play the fish at all. With rod straight ahead, he slowly and steadily reeled in his catch. How he managed to hold the fish was a mystery.

Pretty soon the fish was directly below the end of the rod, but the amateur did not stop.

He continued to reel and reel, and, just as the observer reached the water's edge, the fish's head touched the tip. Then the fisherman actually tried to pull his catch through the ring. He did not, of course, succeed.

"What shall I do now?" he asked of the amused Kentuckian on the bank.

"About the only thing you can do now," said the latter, "is to climb up the pole after the fish."

A young man was deeply in love with a beautiful girl. One day she told him that the next day would be her birthday, and he laughingly said that he would send her a bunch of roses, one for each year of her life.

That evening he wrote to his florist, ordering twenty-four roses to be sent the young woman on the first delivery the next day.

The proprietor of the flower shop, looking over the mail in the morning, saw the order and said to the foreman:

"John, here's an order from young Mr. Flint for twenty-four roses. He's a mighty good customer, so put in a dozen extra ones."

And the young man never knew what made the girl so angry with him.

Mrs. O'Flarity is a scrub la
been absent from her duties f
Upon her return her employe
reason for her absence.

"Sure, I've bin carin' for
children," she replied.

"And how many children
O'Flarity?" he asked.

"Siven in all," she replied.
third wife of me second hus
the second wife of me furst."

ges, drums and n
geworldusa.com
RY TO QUALIFIED BUSIN
HELP PRESERVE THE EARTH'S LIMIT

Murphy was a new cavalry
given one of the worst horse

"Remember," said the ser
is allowed to dismount witho

Murphy was no sooner in the saddle than
the horse kicked and Murphy went over his
head.

"Murphy," yelled the sergeant, when he
discovered him lying breathless on the
ground, "you dismounted!"

"I did."

"Did you have orders?"

"I did."

"From headquarters?"

"No, sor; from hindquarters."

The lady had just been introduced to her partner at a holiday dance and was talking to him vivaciously. "Tell me," she said, "who is that terribly homely man over there?"

The gentleman looked. "That," he said ponderously, "is my brother."

"Oh!" gasped the lady in horrified amazement. "Pardon me. Really, I hadn't noticed the resemblance."

Joseph Jefferson was once fishing, when a game warden approached and examined his catch, which consisted of one beautiful black bass. Then the warden said:

"It will cost you, sir, just twenty-five dollars for catching this black bass out of season."

"I take a black bass out of season?" exclaimed Jefferson. "Never! Such an idea never even occurred to me. I'll tell you how it happened," as he handed the warden a cigar. "That black bass was eating the bait off my hooks as fast as I could put it on, so I thought I would just tie him up where he couldn't get at it until I got through fishing."

A woman was discussing the English language with Rudyard Kipling.

" Don't you think it strange, Mr. Kipling," said the woman, with superior wisdom, " that sugar is the only word in the English language where an ' s ' and a ' u ' come together and are pronounced ' sh ' ? "

Mr. Kipling's eyes twinkled as he answered: " Sure."

Richard Butler Glaenzer, the New York essayist and critic, said at the Players Club:

" Poetry is delightful. But poets are so very poorly paid. I know a millionaire who has a beautiful, golden-haired stenographer. The girl said to her employer the other day:

" ' I am going to get married, sir. And I am going to marry a poet.'

" ' Dear me ! ' said the millionaire. ' Then you will leave us, eh ? '

" ' No, sir,' she replied; ' I shall not leave you, but I shall need more pay.' "

Senator Pomerene of Ohio met a friend in front of a bank in Washington one afternoon, and learned a lesson in frenzied finance. The friend was apparently a wretched and miserable man. Woe had claimed him for her own, and anguish was enthroned within his eyes. He was the saddest sight the Senator had ever seen.

"John," said Pomerene with instant sympathy, "you look as if you were in distress."

"I am," and John heaved a windy sigh.

"What's the matter?"

"I'm waiting to get a check cashed."

"Well," exclaimed the Senator in surprise, "why don't you go in and get it cashed? You're standing right in front of a bank."

"But, you see," said John dolefully, "the check won't be any good until the bank closes."

When the Christmas dinner was over the family and the guests adjourned to the big sitting-room, where they were joined by several of the neighbors. Consequently there was a scarcity of chairs, and a young gentleman friend of the family, who had taken dinner with them, took Willie up on his lap.

Then, during a pause in the conversation, little Willie looked up at the young gentleman and piped: "Am I as heavy as sister Mabel?"

" Put down," the little fellow said, reading from a book, " ten pounds of sugar at five cents a pound, an' four pounds of coffee at thirty cents a pound, an' two pounds of butter at twenty-eight cents a pound, an' two cakes of soap at five cents each."

" I've got them down," said the grocer, looking up from his pad.

" How much does it come to? " the lad asked.

The man ran up the column.

" Two-thirty-six," he announced. " Hurry up, son."

" An' if I was to give you a five-dollar bill how much change would I get? "

" Two dollars and sixty-four cents," said the grocer impatiently. " Come on, I'm in a hurry."

" Oh, I didn't want to buy them," said the urchin as he disappeared through the door. " That's our arithmetic lesson for to-morrow an' I couldn't work it."

President Cleveland, while talking to a friend about one of his many angling expeditions, told the following story: " It is remarkable," said the President, " how mean

some people are. I had with me on that particular trip two countrymen who evidently
were familiar with my reputation as an
angler. Before starting one of them made
the following suggestion: 'Mr. President,'
said he, ' we will agree that the first one who
catches a fish must treat the crowd.'

" I assented to this, and we started. Now,
don't you know, those two fellows both had
a bite and were too mean to pull them up."

" I suppose you lost, then," remarked the
friend.

" Oh, no ! " replied the President. " I
didn't have any bait on my hook."

During the Christmas dinner a young
Frenchman was seated next to a fine-looking
young woman who was wearing a gown
which displayed her beautiful arms.

" I came near not being here to-night,"
said she. " I was vaccinated a few days ago
and it gives me considerable annoyance."

The young foreigner gazed at the white
arms of the speaker. " Is that so? " he replied. " Where were you vaccinated? "

The girl smiled demurely and said: " In
Toronto."

Belle and Alice were discussing their sweethearts.

" Alfred, you know, is spending the winter in Florida," said Belle, " and among his Christmas presents he sent me the dearest little alligator you ever saw."

" How lovely," said Alice; " but how are you going to keep him? "

" I hardly know," said Belle, " but I've put him in Florida water until I hear from Alfred."

She came down the street three steps at a time and sailed into the country newspaper office like a whirlwind. She waited for no ceremony, but wildly asked,

" Is this the printin' office? "

" Yes, madam."

" I want to stop my paper."

" All right, madam."

" Stop it right away, too."

" It's stopped," we replied, making a blue line through her husband's name on the subscription list.

" Mebbe that will learn you some hoss sense and how to do the square thing next time, and not to slight people just because

they are poor. If some rich, stuck-up folks
happen to have a bald-headed brat born to
'em, you're in an awful hurry to put it in the
paper and make it out an angel; but when
poor people have a baby, you can't say a
word about it, even if it is the purtiest child
borned. That's what I'm stoppin' the paper
fur. This ort to be a lesson to every paper
in Oklahoma."

And she went out of the office as mad as
a wet hen.

Here's another one about Josephus Dan-
iels:

When he was playing one of the star parts
in the drama of the Baltimore convention last
summer, he was the victim of a catastrophe.
In getting out of his bathtub, he slipped and
injured two of his sturdy and well developed
ribs. When it was announced that he would
be made Secretary of the Navy, one of his
chums from North Carolina asked him one
day:

"How on earth can this country expect its
battleships to be built and boarded by a man
who broke two ribs trying to get out of a
Baltimore bathtub?"

" What did you think of the dinner party last night? "

" It was the most daring bareback perform-ance that I ever attended; and as for your niece, she outstripped all her competitors! "

A clergyman, called suddenly away and unable to officiate at the Christmas services in his own church, intrusted his new curate with the duty. On his return home he asked his wife what she thought of the curate's sermon.

" The poorest I ever heard," she declared; " nothing in it at all."

Later in the day the clergyman, meeting his curate, asked him how he had got along.

" Finely, sir, finely," replied the curate. " I didn't have time to prepare anything my-self, so I preached one of your sermons."

" Speaking of consideration for dumb an-imals," said Congressman John Lawson Bur-nett, of Alabama, in the lobby of a Washing-ton hotel the other day, " I am reminded of a little incident that happened in a town down along the Jersey shore.

" One afternoon a man almost fat enough

to weigh a ton debarked from a train and asked a cabby to drive him to a certain hotel. Reaching the hostelry, the fat man handed the cabby the exact fare and started for the door.

" ' Just a moment, please,' interposed the cabby, looking first at the coin in his hand and then at the man. ' Would you mind stepping back the other way a few yards? '

" ' What for? ' wonderingly queried the portly passenger.

" ' On account of the horse,' answered the cabby, with a grin of satisfaction. ' I don't want him to see the size of the load he has been dragging all over the town for twenty-five cents.' "

He was the happy father of a very pretty and bright little girl of ten. " Dad," she said to him one evening, when he was reading the paper, " every morning, when I am going to school, the boys catch hold of me and kiss me."

" But, Ethel," he said, " why don't you run away from them? "

" Well, dad, if I did, perhaps they wouldn't chase me."

"Norah," said the mistress, "are these French sardines that you have given me?"

"Shure, Oi don't know, ma'am," said the new cook; "they were pasht spakin' whin we opened the box."

A man from the city went to a small country town in New Hampshire to spend his vacation. At the station he took the stage, which was drawn by two dilapidated horses, and found that he had no smaller bill than a five-dollar one, which he handed to the driver.

The driver looked at it for a moment or so, and then said: "Which horse do you want?"

"Miss Hunt, I love you, but now I dare not dream of calling you mine. Yesterday I was worth ten thousand dollars, but to-day, by a turn of fortune's wheel, I have but a few paltry hundreds to call my own. I would not ask you to accept me in my reduced state. Farewell forever."

"Good gracious! Reduced from ten thousand dollars to one hundred dollars! What a bargain! Of course I'll take you! You might have known I couldn't resist!"

"Aren't you pretty young to be a practicing physician?" asked the severe-looking female person sternly.

"Well, you see, I only doctor children," said the young medico, nervously.

They were speaking of how easy it is to raise a question of doubt in the human mind, the other afternoon, when Senator Thornton, of Louisiana, recalled the skepticism of little Jimmy.

Little Jimmy, the Senator explained, was one of the gladsome youngsters in a Louisiana school. During the exercises recently the teacher told the school the story of the Roman who swam across the Tiber three times before breakfast.

"Three times!" involuntarily said the wondering Jimmy. "Did you say three times, Miss Mary?"

"Why, yes, Jimmy," responded the teacher. "You don't doubt that a trained swimmer could do it, do you?"

"No, ma'am," was the smiling reply of Jimmy. "I just wondered why he didn't make it four and get back to the side where he left his clothes."

Two women met the other day in a fashionable cafe.

"Mrs. Tobey," remarked the first woman, "isn't in your set any more, is she?"

"No, indeed!" replied the other. "She had to drop out of that set."

"Drop out!" exclaimed the first speaker. "Why, she told me she climbed out."

Ellen, Mrs. B.'s cook, had invested several months' savings in an elaborate Easter hat and gown, and had selected her afternoon off as the day in which she should burst forth in all her glory.

Having carefully arrayed herself, and longing for admiration, Ellen made an excuse to go into her mistress's presence, and waited for a compliment.

Knowing what was expected, Mrs. B. exclaimed:

"Why, Ellen, how splendid you are in your new hat and gown! I hope you will meet all your friends this afternoon, so that they may see your fine clothes."

Ellen smiled graciously at the compliment, but tossed her head at the suggestion.

"Me friends, mum? What'll I be wantin'

to see thim for?" she asked scornfully.
"Sure, I don't care to make me friends jealous. It's me enemies I want to meet whin
I'm dressed up!"

"You will forgive me if I — er — ask you
something — something" —
"Sure I will! I knew you would be asking
it soon."
"Ah, you know what I am about to ask
you? Your heart has told you what" —
"Sure! You're going to ask me what time
the last car goes by?"

"When women set out to say mean things
about each other they usually succeed," said
a well-known New York State senator the
other day. "My wife had several guests
recently and I overheard a bit of conversation that I thought was a prize." Then he
told this story:
"A certain Mrs. Blank was under discussion. 'I see that she employs colored help
now,' remarked one of the ladies.
"'Yes,' said another, 'she became tired of
having people ask her if her maids were relatives of the family.'"

" I had always thought the public servants of my own city were the freshest on earth," says a New York man, " but a recent experience in Kansas City has led me to a revision of that notion.

" One afternoon I dashed into a railway station of that town, with just half a minute to buy my ticket and enter a train for Chicago. I dashed through the first gate, and, pointing to a certain train, asked hurriedly of the gateman,

" ' Is that my train? '

" ' Well, I don't know,' replied he, with exasperating deliberation. ' Maybe it is, but the cars have the company's name on them.' "

Meg (five years old) was overjoyed over the recent addition to the family and rushed out of the house to tell the news to a passing neighbor.

" Oh, you don't know what we've got in our house to-day! "

" What is it? "

" It's a new baby brother! "

" You don't say so! Is he going to stay? "

" I guess so," very thoughtfully. " He's got his things off."

" Mazie Gayway says she makes her husband pay her a dollar every time he kisses her. She's saving for a limousine."

" Now, if she'd only adopted a similar plan before she met Gayway, she might have had a whole garage."

The president of a college was visiting the little town that had been his former home and had been asked to address an audience of his former neighbors. In order to assure them that his career had not caused him to put on airs, he began his address thus:

" My dear friends — I won't call you ladies and gentlemen — I know you too well to say that."

Mrs. Kate Douglas Wiggin, addressing the students of Smith College, told a story.

" A young man," she said, " fell upon his left knee, clasped his hands and cried:

" ' Miss McClintock — Mabel — if you refuse me, I shall never love another woman.'

" ' And does that promise hold good,' said the young girl, ' if I accept you?' "

The teacher was hearing the youthful class in mathematics.

" No," she said, " in order to subtract things have to be in the same denomination. For instance, we couldn't take three pears from four peaches, nor eight horses from ten cats. Do you understand? "

There was assent from the majority of pupils. One little boy in the rear raised a timid hand.

" Well, Bobby, what is it? " asked the teacher.

" Please, teacher," said Bobby, " couldn't you take three quarts of milk from two cows? "

When the suffragettes had special headquarters in Washington last February preparatory for their grand parade the day before the inauguration of Woodrow Wilson, newspaper correspondents thronged the rooms in the hope of getting " human interest " stories every day.

One morning Norborne Robinson, representative of a Boston paper, dropped in and found that the human interest supply had been exhausted. " By the way," he suggested casually, " how about that story that Annette Kellermann is going to put on her famous diving suit and ride in the parade as Lady Godiva ? "

After which Mr. Robinson did a spiral dive down the stairway.

A Washington official who is noted for his skill at whist one evening met a young woman who evinced great curiosity as to the number of prizes he had taken at tournaments.

" And do you really enjoy whist ? " she finally asked.

The expert seemed surprised by the query. " Not at all, young lady," he responded. " I play a distinctly scientific game, you know."

At a dinner in New York, James Montgomery Flagg, the clever artist, told this story to illustrate the influence of the artistic atmosphere :

" You can't escape the artistic atmosphere. Even my cook cannot escape it. She came into the studio to-day, and said: ' About the potatoes for lunch, sir — will you have them in their jackets or in the nood? ' "

He was just about exasperated with the telephone, was Mr. Busiman. Ten times that morning he had tried to get on to a number, and each time something had prevented him from speaking. Either it was " number engaged " or the person he wanted to speak to was out or else had denly cut off. At last he got throu

"Halloa!" said he. "Is there?"

"Yes," replied a voice. "Do to speak to him?"

That was the last straw. Bac reply, in icy tones: —

"Oh, no! Nothing of the sort rang up to hand him a cigar!"

This note was sent to a teacher by to explain her son's absence from sc

"DEAR MUM: Please excuse J day. He will not be at school. H as timekeeper for his father. Last gave him this iximple. If a field is square how long will it take a ma three miles an hour to walk two times around it? Johnny ain't no man, so we had to send his daddy. They left early this morning, and my husband said they ought to be back late to-night, tho it would be hard going. Dear Mum, please make the nixt problem about ladies, as my husband can't afford to lose the day's work. I don't have no time to loaf, but I can spare a day off occasionally better than my husband can.

     " Resp'y yrs,
       " Mrs. Jones."

"You must not eat any more to-night, Willie," said his mother. " Don't you know you can't sleep on a full stomach?"

"That's all right, mamma," replied the youngster. " I can sleep on my back."

"Now, children," said the visiting minister who had been asked to question the Sunday-school, " with what did Samson arm himself to fight against the Philistines?"

None of the children could tell him.

"Oh, yes, you know!" he said, and to help them he tapped his jaw with one finger. "What is this?" he asked.

This jogged their memories, and the class cried in chorus: " The jawbone of an ass."

Governor Hadley, of Missouri, is much interested in gardening and loves to work in his own garden during the summer. He was recently speaking of amateur gardening and the woes of the amateur in trying to make things grow, which, while very amusing to others are decidedly real to himself.

"A young man of my acquaintance," relates the Governor, "was married last spring, and moved to a suburban place, mainly with the idea of being able to have fresh, home-grown vegetables from his own garden.

"Every evening he would hurry through his dinner, rush out to his garden and expend much energy thereon. When the tiny green things began to come up in his neighbors' gardens, his remained as bare as Sahara.

"'I can't understand it,' he confided to me, one evening. 'Not one blessed thing has made an appearance. I planted corn and beans and tomatoes.'

"'Well,' I replied, trying to think of a reason why this should be, 'perhaps the seed you used were defective.'

"'It couldn't have been that,' he said, earnestly, 'for I bought the very best, regardless of price. Why, I paid eighteen cents a can for all of them.'"

BUY 2 INK REFILLS & GET 3RD FREE WITH EXCHANGE

Not valid with any other offers.
3rd cartridge of equal or lesser value.
In store purchases only. Expires 5/31/08.

MAY 08   F1,2,3,4   M1,2   SD0805 076

"Dear Clara," wrote the young man, "pardon me, but I'm getting so forgetful! I proposed to you last night, but really forgot whether you said yes or no."

"Dear Will," she replied by note, "so glad to hear from you! I knew that I said no to some one last night, but I had forgotten who it was."

Pat, Mike and Terry went to war. During a battle Mike's arm was shot off. Running to Pat he cried: "Oh, Pat, Oi've had me ar-rm shot off."

Pat turned to him in disgust.

"Quit yer howlin'. Look at Terry over there. He's had his head shot off an' he ain't sayin' a word."

The city girl boarding in the country spoke to the farmer about the savage way in which the cow regarded her.

"Well," said the farmer, "it must be on account of that red waist you're wearing."

"Dear me," said the girl; "of course I know it's awfully out of fashion, but I had no idea a country cow would notice it."

When the iceman came out of the house he found a small boy sitting on one of his blocks of ice. " 'Ere," he roared, " wot are yer a-sitting on that for? Git off of it!"

The small boy raised a tear-stained face. " Was you ever a boy?" he queried faintly.

" Of course I was," said the iceman, fuming. " But —"

" And did you never play truant?" cut in the youngster.

" Of course I did," snarled the iceman. " Now then you —"

" An' when you got home did yer father take a stick an' —"

" Sit where you are, my little man," the iceman said, gulping. " I understand."

The Wheatons had amassed a vast fortune within the past few years and rose from obscurity to an enviable position in society. The daughters of the household, however, had never been able to successfully " polish " mother to their exacting ideas, and oftentimes her remarks were a trial to their otherwise blissful existence.

One evening they were entertaining a party of friends at dinner and conversation turned

to music. Then mother strove to remember
the name of a certain composer.

" I can't remember it to save my life," she
remarked, after meditating deeply for a few
moments, " and there it was at my tongue's
end a moment ago. As near as I can come
to it, his name is Doorknob."

The girls looked aghast at each other, and
one of them said quietly:

" You mistake, mother; there is no composer whose name sounds anything like doorknob."

Then wishing to make up for her mother's
deficient knowledge on the subject, she said:

" I will go over a few names: Beethoven,
Mendelssohn, Wagner, Haydn, Handel — "

" That's it! " interrupted mother. " It's
Handel. I knew it was something you seized
with your hands."

Two chance acquaintances from Ireland
were talking together.

" An' so yer name is Riley? " said one.
" Are yez anny relation to Tim Riley? "

" Very dishtantly," said the other. " Oi
wus me mother's first child, an' Tim was the
twelfth."

Talking of the frenzied finance agitation that has been going the rounds lately, a Washington official tells how a constituent of his out in California manages to do things.

This friend bought a new auto and mortgaged his home to pay for it. Then he built a garage.

"How are you going to pay for the garage?" asked a friend.

"Cinch," said the other; "I've mortgaged the car."

"But what'll you do when these mortgages fall due?" persisted the friend.

"Easy," replied the frenzied financier. "Then I'll mortgage the garage."

A stunning specimen of the Princeton Tiger was fondly holding the hand of the pretty little Vassar lass, and at last he approached the leading subject courageously. "I have carefully studied the matter from the scientific point of view, and am thoroughly convinced that we are fitted one for the other."

"Please explain yourself," said she, looking up at him with her large, bright eyes.

"It is simply this," he continued, " according to science, which is the only way to approach the subject. You see, you are light and I am dark. You are short and I am tall. You are small and I am large and powerful. You are sprightly, vivacious; I am somewhat sober and phlegmatic. In short, we are opposites, and opposites should marry."

"Yes," she replied; "but there are exceptions to all such rules, and I know of one in this case that is sufficient. I cannot marry you."

"In what respect is this exception made?" he demanded excitedly.

"You see," she smiled up at him again, "you are like me in this: I could never earn my own living."

"Doctor, this bill is exorbitant and I won't pay it," said the patient irritably. "Besides I'm no better than I was before I came to you anyway."

"Of course you're no better," retorted the physician, "and all because you didn't take my advice."

"Oh!" said the patient. "Of course, as I didn't take it I don't owe you anything for it. Good evening."

Ordinarily, the members of the House are anxious to do anything in their power for their constituents and to be as polite as possible about it. But once in awhile the rule is broken. An office seeker was trying to persuade a Southern member that, as a hard-working political lieutenant, he should be rewarded with a piece of the government payroll.

" There's no use in talking about it ! " exclaimed the Congressman roughly. " You're not competent to fill these jobs up here."

The constituent, insulted by the tone, more than the matter, of the remark, turned immediately to go out of the office.

" Wait a minute ! " called the lawmaker, realizing that he had been impolite, and reaching for a printed document on his desk. " Have you read my last speech? "

Replied the job seeker with beautiful contempt, " I hope I have ! "

A newcomer in a Nevada mining district tells an anecdote that admirably illustrates the extreme caution of the Western man regarding any controversy.

The new arrival met an interesting young

stranger, and, as it was near night, proposed that they pitch camp together. After they had unpacked their things and had a bite to eat, they were enjoying a quiet smoke prior to retiring.

The newcomer ventured to remark, " Fine night."

" Looks like rain," observed the other.

" Oh, no, I don't think so."

Whereupon the young Westerner, to his companion's great astonishment, got up and deliberately began packing his kit.

" What's the matter? "

" Oh, I guess I'd better move on."

" But why? "

" Too much argument."

Reports had come to the president of a famous Eastern college that one of the students was drinking more than was good for him. Meeting the offender on the campus one morning the head of the university stopped him and said severely:

" Young man, do you drink? "

" Well — why " — the student hesitated — " not so early in the morning, thank you, Doctor."

" My wife," said Mr. Clarke, " sent two dollars in answer to an advertisement of a sure method of getting rid of superfluous fat."

" And what did she get for the money? Was the information what she wanted? " asked Mr. Simmons.

" Well, she got a reply telling her to sell it to the soap man."

Among the members of a working gang on a certain railroad was an Irishman who claimed to be very good at figures. The boss, thinking that he would get ahead of Pat, said: " Say, Pat, how many shirts can you get out of a yard? "

" That depinds," answered Pat, " on whose yard you get into."

" My father and I know everything in the world," said a small boy to his companion.

" All right," said the latter. " Where's Asia? "

It was a stiff question, but the little fellow answered coolly: " That is one of the questions my father knows."

A little girl was reading a composition of her own on "Grant's Work in the Civil War." She got on swimmingly until she reached Lee's surrender at Appomattox Court House. Then she told how Lee wore his sword and was handsomely attired in full uniform; "while Grant," she announced, "had on nothing but an old, ragged union suit."

It was the first of April.

"Mamma! Mamma!" came a piping treble, "come quick; there's a strange man in the dining-room kissing the waitress."

The mother made a hurried start, but was halted by her gay little son, who cried exultingly: "April Fool! It's only Papa!"

When the young physician's automobile reached the scene of the trolley accident there was nothing to do; all the victims had been so slightly hurt that they were able to walk home. The young doctor was keenly disappointed, but his chauffeur spoke up cheeringly:

"Never mind, Doctor. I'll run down some business on the way home."

" I so admire a man who, like your husband, always dresses so quietly," said Mrs.
Smith to Mrs. Jones.

" Oh, no, he doesn't," said Mrs. Jones.
" You ought to hear him when he loses a
collar-button."

A woman was in a law court when she was
asked her age, and answered: " Thirty-five."

" But," objected the Judge, " you were before me two years ago, and you said then
that you were thirty-five."

" Your Honor," she loftily replied, " I am
not one who would say one thing at one time
and another thing at another time."

He had an invariable way of asking the
wrong question or making the wrong com-
ment. So it was, when at a dinner party his
neighbor, a lady, said to him: " I am a thor-
ough believer, you know, Mr. Smith, that
men's clothes should match their hair; a
black-haired man should wear black clothes,
a brown-haired man should wear brown
clothes. Don't you think so? "

" That may be," bungled Jones, " but suppose a man is bald? "

At the wedding reception the young man remarked: " Wasn't it annoying the way that baby cried during the whole ceremony? "

" It was simply dreadful," replied the prim little maid of honor; " and when *I* get married I'm going to have engraved right in the corner of the invitations: ' No babies expected.' "

A clergyman who advertised for an organist received this reply:

" DEAR SIR: I notice you have a vacancy for an organist and music teacher, either lady or gentleman. Having been both for several years I beg to apply for the position."

At the close of his talk before a Sunday-school the Bishop invited questions.

A tiny boy, with white, eager face, at once held up his hand. " Please, sir," said he, " why was Adam never a baby? "

The Bishop coughed in doubt as to what answer to give, but a little girl, the eldest of several brothers and sisters, came promptly to his aid.

" Please, sir," she answered smartly, " there was nobody to nuss him."

"My dear," said the professor's wife, "the hens have scratched up all that eggplant seed you sowed."

"Ah! jealousy!" mused the professor. And he sat down and wrote a twenty-page article on the "Development of Envy in the Minds of the Lower Bipeds."

"Here, Alfred, is an apple. Divide it politely with your little sister."

"How shall I divide it politely, Mamma?"

"Why, always give the larger part to the other person, my child."

Alfred thought a moment, then handed the apple to his little sister, saying: "Here, Sis, you divide it."

"Want a job, eh?" said the prospective employer to the shrewd-looking applicant for the position as errand boy. "Well, do you know how far the moon is from the earth?"

"Naw, sir," said the youth, "I don't know. But it ain't close enough to prevent me from runnin' yer errands."

He got the job.

A little Scotch boy had just returned from a painful interview with the minister, to whom he had said, in reply to a question, that there were one hundred Commandments. Meeting another lad on his way to the minister's he asked: " An' if he asks ye how mony Commandments there are, what will ye say ? "

" Say ? " replied the other boy; " why, ten, of course."

" Ten? " said the first urchin in scorn. " Ten? Ye wull try him wi' ten? I tried him wi' a hundred and he wasna satisfied."

She walked into the public library and sweetly said:

" I would like ' The Red Boat,' please."

The librarian diligently searched the catalogue, and came back with:

" I don't think we have such a book."

Flushing a bit she sweetly said: " May the title be ' The Scarlet Yacht '? "

Again he looked, with the same result. Then with her pretty fingers she went into her bag, consulted a slip of paper and said:

" Oh, I beg pardon. I mean the ' Rubaiyat.' "

The automobile was a thing unheard of to a mountaineer in one community, and he was very much astonished one day when he saw one go by without any visible means of loco-motion. His eyes bulged, however, when a motorcycle followed closely in its wake and disappeared like a flash around a bend in the road.

" Gee whiz ! " he said, turning to his son, " who'd 'a' s'posed that thing had a colt ? "

When the Reverend John McNeil was holding revival services at Cardiff a young man one night, thinking to perplex the preacher, sent up a note to the platform with the request that the following question might be publicly answered:

" Dear Mr. McNeil — If you are seeking to enlighten young men kindly tell me who was Cain's wife."

Mr. McNeil read the note, and then, amid breathless silence, said:

" I love young men — inquirers for truth especially — and should like to give this young man a word of advice. It is this: Don't lose your soul's salvation looking after other people's wives."

" What is it, children? " asked the superintendent, " that binds us together and makes us better than we are by nature? Who can tell? "

Little Ellen Smith's hand shot up.

" Yes, Ellen; can you tell? "

" Yes, sir; corsets."

" You don't make very good music with that instrument." said a bystander to the man with the bass drum, as the band ceased to play.

" No," admitted the pounder of the drum, " I know I don't; but I drown a heap of bad music."

Two hard citizens were standing in a secluded spot talking confidentially. One of them suddenly sneaked away while the other stood on guard Soon the first one was seen to emerge from a window and join his pal.

" Did youse git anyt'ing? " whispered the one in waiting

" Naw, de guy what lives in dere is a lawyer," growled the other.

" Dat's hard luck," said his pal. " Did youse lose anything? "

A gentleman who was continually losing his collar-button while dressing complained to his wife about it. With an ingenuity born of the use of hairpins she told him to hold his collar-button in his mouth and he wouldn't lose it. This worked for several days, when one morning she was startled by an unusual commotion.

"What's the matter?" asked the wife anxiously.

"I've swallowed the collar-button," said the man.

"Well," responded his better half, "for once in your life you know where it is."

Captain Coffin, one of the old-time whalers of Nantucket, had a thrilling experience with a big sperm whale in the south Pacific. He had fairly harpooned the whale, when the monster turned, crushing the boat in its enormous jaws, and scattering the crew into the waves.

The captain found himself in the whale's jaws, but managed to wriggle out, and was rescued with his men, luckily uninjured.

"Captain Con," said a solemn friend, when the old sailor was relating the adventure, "what did you think when you were in the jaws of that great whale?"

"Think!" said the captain. "Why, I thought he'd make a hundred barrels — and he did."

"This," said the dealer, "is the best automobile you could buy; just the thing for a lady."

"Really?" remarked Miss Bright; "I suppose it's — er — kind and gentle and not afraid of electric cars."

A farmer, buying some tools in a hardware store, was asked by the proprietor if he did not want to buy a bicycle.

"A bicycle won't eat its head off," said the salesman, "and you can ride it around your farm. They're cheap now and I can let you have one for thirty-five dollars."

"I guess I'd ruther put the thirty-five into a cow," said the farmer reflectively.

"Ha-ha," laughed the hardware man, "you'd look mighty foolish, riding round your farm on a cow, now, wouldn't you?"

"Well, I dunno," said the farmer, "no more foolish than I would milking a bicycle."

They were giving a big dinner, and the coachman had come in to help wait on the table. Several persons had suffered from his lack of experience, and in serving peas he approached a very deaf old lady and inquired:

" Peas, mum? "

No answer.

" Peas, mum? " (Louder.)

The old lady saw that some one was speaking to her, and she lifted her ear trumpet to the questioner. The coachman, seeing the large end of the trumpet directed toward him, thought:

" It must be a new way o' takin' 'em, but I s'pose she likes 'em that way."

And down the trumpet went the peas.

A Colorado man who is visiting in Wellington told H. L. Woods this story: " The game warden of Colorado was walking out in the mountains the other day when he met a hunter with his gun. The officer suggested that that ought to be a good country for hunting.

" It certainly is," said the hunter proudly. " I killed one of the finest bucks yesterday I ever saw, and he weighed over 200." It was the season when deer may not be shot without subjecting the hunter to a heavy fine.

" Well, that is a fine one," said the warden, " and do you know who you are talking to? "

Being assured that he did not the officer said:

" Why, I am the chief game warden of Colorado."

The hunter was only taken back a moment, when he said:

" And do you know who you are talking to? " The warden did not know.

" Well, sir," said the hunter, apparently much relieved, " you are talking to the biggest liar in the whole state of Colorado."

The young lawyer didn't like the minister, and so he thought to corner him. " Now, Doctor," he asked, " suppose the parsons and the devil should have a lawsuit, which party do you think would win? "

" The devil unquestionably," replied the minister.

" Ah? " chuckled the young lawyer. " And will you tell us why? "

" Because he would have all the lawyers on his side."

He was a young lawyer who had just started practicing in a small town and hung his sign outside his office door. It read: " A. Swindler." A stranger who called to consult him saw the sign and said: " My goodness, man, look at that sign! Don't you see how it reads? Put in your first name — Alexander, Ambrose or whatever it is."

" Oh, yes, I know," said the lawyer resignedly, " but I don't exactly like to do it."

" Why not? " asked the client. " It looks mighty bad as it is. What is your first name? "

" Adam."

William Jennings Bryan tells a good story, at his own expense, of a time when he was not as well known as he is now.

A widely admired campaign speaker in Nebraska, who had been billed to make the principal address at a political gathering in Lincoln, was obliged, at the last moment, on account of illness, to send word that he could not keep the appointment. It chanced that Mr. Bryan was selected to fill his place. Naturally, Mr. Bryan felt some nervousness, knowing that he was to act as substitute for an older, and much better known speaker, and his apprehension was not lessened when he heard himself thus announced by the chairman:

"Feller citizens, this here's the substitute for our gallant an' admired leader, unfortunately sick. I don't know what this gent can do; but time was short an' we had to take what we could git."

Mark Twain and Dan De Quille roomed together in early Comstock days. One morning Dan missed his boots, and after a vain search he suspiciously inquired of Mark, who was lying in bed lazily smoking a clay pipe: "Mark, I can't find my boots; do you know anything about 'em?" "Your boots," complacently replied Mark. "Well yes; I threw them at the blasted cat that was yelling around the house last night!" "Threw my boots at the cat?" howled Dan, in a rage. "Why didn't you throw your own boots!"

"Dan," said Mark, after a reflective puff or two, "if there is anything I hate, it is a selfish man. I have observed of late that you are growing selfish. What difference does it make whose boots are thrown at the cat?"

An old man was talking to a bachelor and asked him why he did not marry. He parried the question by telling about different young women he had known, finding some fault with each one. But it appeared that all of them had married.

" You are in danger of getting left," said the old man to him. " You had better hurry up before it is too late."

" Oh," said the bachelor, " there are just as many good fish left in the sea."

" I know that," replied the old man, " but the bait — isn't there danger of the bait becoming stale ? "

This is the way the little Boston girls sing, " I Don't Want to Play in Your Yard : "

" I have no desire for amusement within the curtilege of your residence.

" I am averse to the personality which erstwhile was a source of gratification to me.

" A sentiment of regret will pervade your being, upon observing my method of locomotion, in descending the covered aperture leading to your subway.

" It will be impossible for you to vocalize effectively down the subterranean passage which is utilized as a receptacle for the showers of early spring.

"I shall not permit the ascent of the apple tree which is owned in fee simple by myself and family.

"I reiterate. I have no wish to play around the adjacent parts of your premises,

"Unless I am accorded the respect which is commensurate with my station in life."

"What you need, Madam," said the physician to his fashionable lady patient, "is oxygen. Come every afternoon for your inhalations. They will cost you five dollars each."

"There," said the lady, "I just knew that other doctor didn't know his business. He told me all I needed was plain fresh air."

"Are you the judge of reprobates?" said Mrs. Partington, as she walked into an office of a judge of probate.

"I am a judge of probate," was the reply.

"Well, that's as I expected," quoth the old lady. "You see my father died detested and left several little infants, and I want to be their executioner."

A curious person of a certain town, who loved to find out everything about the new residents, espied the son of a new neighbor one morning, in a doctor's office.

"Good-morning," he said. "Little boy, what is your name?"

"Same as dad's," was the quick reply.

"Of course, I know, little boy, but what is your dad's name, dear?"

"Same as mine, sir."

Still he persisted: "I mean what do they say when they call you to breakfast?"

"They don't never call me; I allus gets there first."

"Interim," explained the teacher, "is that which follows one event and precedes another. Now I would like to have each member of the class compose a sentence containing the word 'interim' and read it when we have our recitation to-morrow."

Little Willie was the first to be asked for his composition on the following day. It was as follows:

"When Charlie Bronson come to our house to see Sister Helen the other nite, pa went down stairs and told him to git out, but he took hold of Helen's hand and they both looked at pa and said they wouldn't ever part no more. So pa got in front of one event and followed the other toward the door and threw the boots interim."

The class was dismissed without any further reports.

A negro was brought up before the Mayor of Philadelphia, a short time since, for stealing chickens.

"Well, Toby," said his honor, "what have you to say for yourself?"

"Nuffin' but dis, boss, I was as crazy as a bedbug when I stole dat ar' pullet, coz I might hab stole de big rooster, and neber done it. Dat shows 'clusively to my mind dat I was laboring under de delirium tremendous."

An old Georgia negro having told the judge that he had "been in three wars," was asked to name them, when he replied: "I wuz a cook in de confedrit war, an' atter freedom broke out I wuz married two times!"

An old gentleman, rather portly and clad in a somewhat youthful suit of light gray flannel, sat on a bench in the park enjoying the spring day.

"What's the matter, sonny?" he asked a small urchin who lay on the grass just across the walk and stared intently. "Why don't you go and play?"

"Don't wanter," the boy replied.

"But it is not natural," the old gentleman insisted, "for a boy to be so quiet. Why don't you run about?"

"Oh; I'm just waitin'," the little fellow answered. "I'm just waitin' till you get up. A man painted that bench about fifteen minutes ago."

A bashful cowboy, returning from the plains to civilized society after an absence of several years, fell desperately in love at first sight with a pretty young girl whom he met at a party.

On leaving the house that evening the young lady forgot her overshoes, and the hostess, who had noticed the Westerner's infatuation, told the young Lochinvar that he might return them to the girl if he wished.

The herder leaped at the chance and presented himself in due time at the young lady's house. She greeted him cordially.

"You forgot your overshoes last night," he said, awkwardly handing her the package.

"Why, there's only one overshoe here!" she exclaimed, as she thanked him and opened it.

"Yes, Miss," said he, blushing. "I'll bring the other one to-morrow. Oh, how I wish that you were a centipede!" And with that he turned and sped away down the street.

A colored gentleman recently asked his employer to be let off early on a certain day.

"Someone ill?" he was asked.

"No, suh! de society what I b'longs ter is holdin' of a reception to a gentleman what we ain't see in some time."

"What gentleman?"

"Hit's a gentleman, suh," was the reply, "what is des got back from spendin' some time in Dade County."

"What's his business?"

"He was in the burglary business, suh, but he got kotched."

Potter Palmer, hearing of the whereabouts of a guest who had decamped from the Palmer House without going through the formality of paying his bill, sent him a note:

" Mr. ——, Dear Sir: Will you send amount of your bill, and oblige," etc.

To which the delinquent replied:

" The amount is $8.62. Yours respectfully."

A Washington artist, while sketching in North Carolina, was one day in search of a suitable background of dark pines for a picture he had planned. At last he found the precise situation he was seeking, and, best of all, there chanced to be a pretty detail in the figure of an old colored woman in the foreground.

The artist asked the old woman to remain seated until he had sketched her. She assented with the greatest good-nature; but in a few minutes asked how long the artist would be.

" Oh, only about a quarter of an hour," he answered.

Three minutes or so later the old darkey again inquired — this time with manifest anxiety — how long the operation of sketching would take.

"Not long," was the reassuring reply; "but why do you ask so anxiously?"

"Oh, nuthin', sah," the old woman hastened to respond, "only, I's sittin' on an ant-hill, sah."

While visiting the South, recently, a traveler chanced upon a resident of a sleepy hamlet in Alabama.

"Are you a native of this town?" asked the traveler.

"Am I what?" languidly asked the one addressed.

"Are you a native of the town?"

"What's that?"

"I asked you whether you were a native of the place?"

At this juncture there appeared at the open door of the cabin the man's wife, tall, sallow, and gaunt. After a careful survey of the questioner, she said:

"Ain't you got no sense, Bill? He means was yo' livin' heah when you was born, or was yo' born before yo' begun livin' heah. Now answer him."

The difference between an accident and a misfortune has been defined thus: Suppose you walk along the bank of a river in company with your mother-in-law. If she should fall into the water and be drowned, it is an accident; if she should fall into the water and be pulled out alive, it is a misfortune.

Adam, they say, must have been a happy man: he had no mother-in-law.

Among the stories in " Pages From an Adventurous Life," by Mr. J. E. Preston-Muddock, is one that Lord Alverstone was wont to tell with appreciation. In a post-office prosecution at Hertford assizes a clever Irish barrister appeared for the defendant, who was a poor letter-carrier guilty of some irregularity. Among the witnesses was Anthony Trollope, then government post-office inspector. After he had given his testimony he was handed over to the lawyer for his defense for cross-examination.

"What are you?" demanded the keen Irishman, in a severe and commanding tone, sonorous with a rich brogue.

"An official in the post-office," answered

Trollope, somewhat astonished by the lawyer's brusqueness.

"Anything else?" demanded the cross-examiner, with a snap.

"Yes; an author." This a little proudly.

"What is the name of your last book?"

"'Barchester Towers.'"

"Now tell me, is there a word of truth in that book?"

"Well, it is what is generally called a work of fiction."

"Fiction!" with a scornful curl of the lip. "Fiction! That is to say, there isn't a word of truth in it from beginning to end?"

"I — I am afraid, if you put it that way, there isn't," stammered Trollope, in an embarrassed way.

With a triumphant air the lawyer turned to the jury.

"Gentlemen," he exclaimed, "how can you possibly convict a man on the evidence of a witness like this, who here in this court of justice unblushingly confesses that he has written a book in which there is not one word of truth!"

Trollope had fallen squarely into the pit digged for him by his unscrupulous cross-examiner.

The late Tom L. Johnson's fame as a public speaker still lives throughout the United States; but behind his reputation for oratory was a tragedy.

He was thirty-four years old when he made his first public speech, and on that occasion, as he said afterward, he died a thousand deaths, lost all his vocabulary, and divorced himself from every idea. When the speech was over, he sought to comfort himself by asking the opinion of a friend who had heard his remarks.

" How was that speech? " was his inquiry.

" It was," replied the comforter, " the worst I ever heard."

There is a certain Western Congressman, a golf enthusiast, who, when he came to Washington for the first time, was accustomed to get to the Chevy Chase Club's links early in the morning, when there would be no one to witness his lack of skill.

On one occasion a caddie had followed him to the tee and offered to go the course with him for the modest compensation of fifty cents.

" I don't need you, my boy," said the

Representative. " I'll go it alone," and as he spoke the Westerner, making a tremendous swipe at the ball, missed it by a foot.

" I'll go round with you for a quarter, sir," said the caddie.

Again the amateur declined the caddie's attendance; and again he swung at the ball with the same result.

" I'll go with you for fifteen cents," said the boy.

This so rattled the newcomer that he made three more wild swings. The caddie, as he retreated a bit, called out:

" Say, mister, won't you take me round for nothing? I'll go for the fun of it."

Out in the West, a sable knight of the lather and brush was performing the operation of shaving a customer with a very dull razor.

" Stop," said the customer, " that won't do."

" What's de matter, boss? "

" The razor pulls."

" Well, no matter for dat, sah. If de handle ob de razor don't break, de beard's bound to come off."

A little fellow swallowed a penny. Imme-diately on getting the information, the mother-in-law wrote to her son-in-law, in-quiring, "Has Ernest got over his financial difficulties yet?"

Opie Read tells a good barber story on himself. He had just returned from Hot Springs, Ark., and on his way home stopped at a little place in Mississippi called Hamp-ton. He wanted to get shaved, and was di-rected to a shop kept by a colored man. Opie went in, looked around the shanty and saw a wooden arm-chair, with a crutch nailed on the back for a head-rest. He hesitated about getting in, and asked the barber if it was all right.

"Yas, sir; yas, sir; shaved heap er smart men in dar, sir!"

Opie seated himself. The barber reached down and took out his razor and began sharpening it on his boot. "Look here, my friend," said Read, "are you sure you have shaved any white people before?"

"Kaws I hez, baws. Don't git skeert. Jess set right still."

Opie looked all around the shop. There

wasn't a sign of a brush or any kind of a tool anywhere. Having honed the razor to his satisfaction the barber strapped it off on a twelve-foot cornstalk that stood in one corner. Then he stooped down and fished out a pan of soft soap, which was hid under the operating chair, and taking a supply on each hand he dabbed the stuff on his customer's face and rubbed it very vigorously.

Opie groaned, but it was too late to withdraw. Every time the razor touched his cheek some hogs which were rooting below, would hunch up their backs against the underpinning and shake the entire building; consequently the barber's hand was none too steady. What Mr. Read suffered will never be made public, for it was agreed when he told the story that the reporter should keep the veil drawn over this portion of the harrowing tale.

A husband, whose mother-in-law was uncongenial, received the following telegram from his wife, " Mother dead. Shall we have her embalmed, cremated, or buried? "

The husband wired back, " Do the three; take no chances."

Sardou, in " Seraphine," says, " If you ever have to choose between living with your mother-in-law or shooting yourself, do not hesitate a single moment — shoot her."

Mandy Spillers, a colored lady, swore out a warrant against Zeb Snow.

" What did this man do? " the justice of the peace asked.

" He 'sulted me, sah; dat's whut he done."

" How — what did he say? "

" Didn't say nuthin'."

" How, then, did he insult you? "

" W'y, sah, he come erlong whar I wuz sweepin' de yard an' grabbed me an' kissed me, he did."

" Did you make an outcry? "

" No, sah."

" Did you try to get away from him? "

" Who, me? Look yere, jedge, do you think good lookin' men is so plenty deze days dat I gwine ter git away from one when he grab me? "

" But if you were so willing how was it an insult? "

" How wuz it er insult? W'y, sah, he

turned me loose an' went 'cross de yard an'
kissed er black imp o' er lady dat is old enuff
ter be my mammy, sah. Dat's how he
'sulted me."

Nothing suited old Abe Jenkins (or
Uncle Abe, as we boys called him) better,
after his day's work, than to sit in his cozy
nook by the kitchen fire and smoke his old
corn-cob. His wife, on the other hand, liked
excitement, and would take in anything and
everything, from a funeral to a patent-medi-
cine show on the street corner. On one occasion, however, the old lady succeeded in per-
suading Uncle Abe to go with her to see a
phrenologist, whose clever advertising even
interested old Abe a little. The old couple,
arriving a little late, were ushered up into the
front row. Much to the amusement of the
crowd, and especially Mrs. Jenkins, Uncle
Abe was chosen as a subject for the professor
to experiment on.

" And now," said the phrenologist, " Mr.
Jenkins, among many physical discomforts,
you are troubled with cold feet also " ——

" Yes ! " yelled Uncle Abe, looking toward
the front row; " but they are not my own."

A diplomat, sitting between Madame de
Staël and Madame Récamier, said, " Here I
am between wit and beauty."

" Yes," quickly retorted Madame de Staël,
" and without possessing either."

John Hays Hammond was the referee of
the National Press Club debate in which four
of the leading statesmen of the country tried
to decide which constituted the greatest men-
ace to navigation, bow legs or knock knees.
In expressing his conviction that the discussion was entirely futile and unnecessary, he
said it reminded him of the accomplishments
of a Laplander girl who got stranded in the
northern part of Florida.

She applied to the mistress of a house for
work, and was asked what she could do.

" Can you cook? " asked the woman.

" No," replied the Laplander girl.

" Can you clean up? "

" No."

" Can you make beds? "

" No."

" What on earth can you do? "

" Well," said the Laplander with pride,
" I can milk a reindeer."

" This farm for sail," read a sign on a gate-post. A passer-by, hailing a little woman who stood on tiptoe hanging out clothes, asked, " When is this farm going to sail? "

Not at a loss, the old lady promptly replied, " Just as soon as anybody comes who can raise the wind."

Senator W. Murray Crane is thanked in personal letters, and in the minds of many others who do not take the trouble to write, for public literature and government documents. Thousands of these publications are sent out under the frank of the Massachusetts Senator, which means that they go free of postage with the Senator's name stamped in one corner. Senator Crane is chairman of the Committee on Rules and has supervision of the press gallery. That also calls for his name on thousands of envelopes in which newspaper men send out documents of all kinds. Consequently, " W. Murray Crane," in facsimile of the Senator's real signature, goes to every part of the country, bearing with it congressional directories, speeches, public documents, and all kinds of literature turned out at the government printing office.

A Boston woman was arguing with a woman belonging to one of the Knickerbocker families of New York as to which had the nobler ancestry. The Bostonian declared that her ancestors came over in the Mayflower, whereupon the New Yorker remarked superciliously that she was not aware before that there were any steerage passengers on the Mayflower.

When a trust magnate gave his church two tablets of stone, with the Ten Commandments engraved on them, a woman in the church remarked that his reason for giving away the Commandments was that he couldn't keep them.

Oscar W. Towner was a boomer in North Dakota back in the territorial days, and was extensively engaged in raising wheat. One spring he was returning from Missouri to Dakota after one of those seasons when crops had failed and prices had fallen. On the train was a man returning from Florida who was exuberantly enthusiastic over the possibility of fortunes in Florida orange groves. He compared orange growing with wheat raising, and pointed out the profits that would surely follow investments.

Towner listened with interest and, looking far away across the melting snow on the Dakota prairies, said, " A man ought to have a big wheat farm in North Dakota where he can spend his summers, and a big orange grove in Florida where he can spend his winters." And after a pause he added, " And a national bank at St. Louis — so that he could draw both ways."

Day after day during the investigations of campaign contributions there were disputes about what Cornelius N. Bliss said or did, from whom he collected and for what purpose.

" Do you remember," asked Dr. Harvey W. Wiley, " that oft-repeated assertion in ' The Old Homestead,' where the old fellow told many tall stories and clenched them by saying, ' And I could prove it too, if old Bill Jones was alive '? I am thinking how much could be proved in this campaign fund investigation if ' Old Cornelius Bliss was alive.' "

A dilapidated bachelor who retained little but his conceit said to Julia Ward Howe, " It is time now for me to settle down as a married man; but I want so much — I want youth, health, wealth, beauty, grace — "

" Yes," she interrupted sympathetically, " you poor man, you want them all."

A dandy, with more good looks than brains, married a rich and accomplished, but very homely woman. One day he said to her, " My dear, ugly as you are, I love you as well as though you were pretty."

" Thank you, Love. Fool as you are, I love you as well as though you had wit."

Thomas J. Pence, who pulled off a prize piece of work in managing President Wilson's campaign publicity work, dropped into a restaurant in Washington one evening and ordered a watercress sandwich.

The waiter set it before him, the slices of bread being cut very thick and the supply of watercress enormous. Pence regarded it in sadness and silence for at least five minutes.

" Waiter," he said at last in a suave tone,

" when I order a watercress sandwich, it doesn't necessarily mean that I wish a meadow concealed between two loaves of bread."

Helen, Rufus Choate's brilliant daughter, made the remark quoted without credit by Emerson:

" To a woman, the consciousness of being well dressed gives a sense of tranquillity which religion fails to bestow."

Perry Belmont is a man overwhelmed by his own fad. He has a mania for collecting clocks, clocks of all sizes and designs, some small enough to wear as shirtstuds and others big enough to make a cathedral bell sound like an intense and well developed silence.

One day a guest in his house remarked on the beauty of the clocks; but added, " I can't tell what time it is. None of these clocks is running."

" That's true," replied Belmont. " There were so many of them and they ticked so loud that I stopped them all. They were lacerating my nerves."

" Didn't Oliver Goldsmith once live here? " asked the tourist.

" I don't remember the name," said the janitor. " Who was the gent? "

" He was a poet."

" Then it's hardly likely that he ever lived here, sir. We always demand the rent in advance."

Hon. Charles E. Magoon, formerly Governor of Cuba, tells the following story:

" Some years ago when I was practising law in Nebraska, in the days when people were anxious for railroad extension and other forms of development, there came to the State one of those men that have a genius for getting their living easily. He was sleek, well fed, and well dressed, important, and full of business. In a short time he organized a railroad company, — none of your small concerns, but one with a title that was high sounding, like the Midland & Pacific, or something like it.

" The Midland & Pacific procured right of way free, secured free grants for terminals and sidings, turnouts and stations, and also town sites. Legislative charters were granted

and State bonds voted. More than that, every other form of bond was also liberally bestowed. County bonds, city bonds, village bonds, township bonds, school district bonds, in fact every kind of bonds that could be issued, were turned over to the Midland & Pacific and its enterprising promoter.

" Then the railroad itself was bonded for the cost of construction and rolling stock. Stocks equal to the amount of bonds were issued and sold to any person who had the money or could mortgage his property and obtain money.

" Some sort of road was graded, some track was laid, enough to call for the delivery of the securities and insure marketing them. Then the whole thing collapsed. Many suits were instituted, and the promoter was brought into court as a witness.

" ' When did you come to this State? ' he was asked.

" ' Ten years ago,' was the reply.

" ' Why did you come to this State? ' was another question.

" ' To do the people good,' was the rather unctuous reply.

" ' Well, you certainly have,' remarked the attorney."

We are apt to fuss and fret
About the one we didn't get;
But we needn't make such an awful fuss
If the one we didn't want didn't get us.

An Englishman walked up to a market-woman's stand and, pointing to some large watermelons, said, " What! don't you raise any bigger apples than these in America? "

Disdainfully the woman replied, " Apples! Anybody might know you was an Englishman. Them is huckleberries."

A supercilious lawyer, cross-examining a young woman whose testimony was likely to result unfavorably to his client, inquired, " You are married, I believe? "

" No, Sir."

" Oh — only about to be married? "

" No, Sir."

" Only wish to be? "

" Really, I don't know. Would you advise such a step? "

" Oh, certainly! I am a married man myself."

" Is it possible? I never should have thought it. Is your wife deaf or blind? "

A young man poured out a long story of adventure to a Boston woman. Surprised, she asked:

" Did you really do that? "

" I done it," answered the proud young man. He began another narrative, more startling than the first.

When she again expressed her surprise, he said, with inflated chest, " I done it."

" Do you know," remarked the girl, " you remind me strongly of Banquo's Ghost? "

" Why? "

" Don't you remember that Macbeth said to him, ' Thou canst not say, " I did it " ' ? " and the young man wondered why everybody laughed.

" Atkins," said the sergeant angrily, " why haven't you shaved this morning? "

" Ain't I shaved? " asked Atkins, in apparent surprise.

" No, you're not," insisted the sergeant; " and I want to know why."

" Well, you see, sergeant," replied the soldier, " there was a dozen of us using the same mirror, and I must have shaved some other man."

Austin H. McConville, assistant solicitor of the Department of Agriculture, was down in Tennessee during the summer, and when stopping at one of the hotels, perhaps where there had been a strike of waiters, was much annoyed on account of the service in the dining room. His waiter was particularly awkward, stupid, and without the least idea of what was required of him.

"See here, Waiter!" said McConville, with much exasperation, "where were you yesterday?"

"Boss," replied the negro complacently, "I was drivin' a cayrt yisterd'y."

Senator McCumber was not a Bull Mooser, and he could not appreciate the vaudeville performances in conventions where women took a leading part. He was particularly severe in his criticism of the demonstration led by a woman in behalf of Colonel Roosevelt at the Republican convention in Chicago.

"What," he asked in severe tones in the Senate, "would George Washington, Thomas Jefferson, or Alexander Hamilton have thought of a convention where a queen of the footlights was brought in for the purpose of producing a stampede at a supposed psychological moment?"

"I am not entirely familiar," interjected Senator Borah of Idaho, "with all the history of Jefferson and Hamilton as to such things; but my opinion is, from what I have read, that they would have enjoyed it."

The new school-teacher in a rural town gave a boy a question in compound proportion for home work one evening. It included the circumstance of "men working ten hours a day to complete a certain work."

The next morning the teacher, in looking over the little pack of exercises, found this boy's sum wholly unattempted. Calling him to her, she asked why he had not tried to do the sum.

The boy, after considerable fumbling around in his pockets, brought forth a note from his father and handed it to her. Unfolding it, the teacher read:

"Miss — I refuse to let my boy do his sum you give him as it looks to me to be a slur at 8-hour sistum enny sum not more than 8 hours he is welcum to do but not more."

Every politician feels that he is competent to discuss the tariff. Every editor can write on the subject. And yet the most expert tariff makers will confess that they do not know all about it. Oscar W. Underwood, chairman of the Ways and Means Committee, has a formula.

" The tariff is not an exact science," remarked Mr. Underwood. " I have been devoting much of my congressional life to the subject, and find that in writing a tariff bill all you can do is to get all the facts you can, study them as closely as you can, get the best expert opinions you can, and then guess as close as you can."

A fishwife entered a tramcar and thought she recognized another passenger as an acquaintance. Accordingly she bent forward and, with an ingratiating smile, said, " That's you, isn't it? I hardly kent ye."

" Aye, that's me," replied the other; " and that's you, isn't it? How are ye?"

" Oh, A'm nae that bad," was the reply.

After this silence ensued, and the first speaker, on further scrutiny, became convinced that the woman opposite was not an acquaintance, after all. Again she bent forward and, with an apologetic smirk, remarked, " But that's nae you at a' ! "

" Nae," replied the other. " It's nae nane o' us ! "

Vaughn Comfort, interlocutor of Honey Boy George Evans's Minstrels, is circulating this story:

An old rustic, bent and painfully limping, was accosted by a friend, who inquired,

" Hello, Zeb ! What's ailin' ye ? "

" Got a big corn between two toes," said Zeb, " and it hurts somethin' awful ! "

" Lemme see it. Mebbe I kin do ye some good."

" No use, Joe. It's been thataway fer six weeks."

" But it won't do any harm to let me try."

Slowly and tenderly the old man removed his boot.

" Great guns, man ! " the friend exclaimed. " How long did you say you have been suffering ? "

" Jest about six weeks."

" This ain't any corn ! " cried Joe. " It's a collar button ! "

It was at the seashore and they were sitting on the beach, while the moon shone beautifully on the surging waves.

"What effect does a full moon have upon the tide?" she asked, looking sweetly up into his face.

"None," he replied, as he drew closer to her; "but it has considerable effect upon the un-tied."

OLD LADY: Well, here's a shilling for you, my poor man.

TRAMP: A shillin'? Lor' bless yer, Lydy, if there ever was a fallen angel, you're it.

This is selected by *Collier's Weekly* as Secretary Bryan's best story:

"The year after coming to Nebraska, in 1888, I delivered fifty speeches against the Republican candidate for Governor, and in each one made it clear why he should not be elected.

"He was elected, however, by the usual majority.

"On the following St. Patrick's Day I was to make a short speech, and Governor Thayer (whom I had tried to defeat) presided. It was a varied program, consisting of songs and speeches and vaudeville numbers. It was the first time I had been in the presence of the Governor, and I wondered whether he felt any resentment toward me for all the work I had done against him.

"At last my turn was reached. The Governor, having been prompted by another man, arose and said: 'The next person on the program is W. J. Bryan,' and as I came forward he stepped toward me, smiled, and extended his hand. I felt greatly pleased that he did not harbor any resentment against me, and grasped his hand warmly as he drew me toward him and whispered: 'Quick! Do you speak, sing, or dance?'

"He had never even heard of me."

"What is your son doing now?"

"Playing the piano in a moving-picture show."

"I shouldn't think you would want him doing that."

"I don't; but when a chap has a musical education, he's got to do something with it, hasn't he?"

This contribution is very faulty in spots, but we give it as it was postcarded to us:

" In a sweet Ohio village, whose chief industry is tillage, I sought a barber-shop to get my hair cut. I didn't find the hair man, but a note tacked on the chair ran: ' Lam the stovepipe if you want me. Charley Faircut.' So I hit the pipe and waited till a girl came in, who stated: ' Say, paw he's busy now out in the barnyard. He's a-workin' like a fool, clippin' ol' Hank Ramsay's mule. You're the next one; but I'll bet that you'll get darn tired ! ' "

Robert Hill is a genius in the rough. He writes good stories, composes good music, and indulges in gorgeous sartorial effects. Moreover, pertinacity is his name.

In the line of duty he went to see Mr. A. A. Adee, the Assistant Secretary of State, who knows all there is to know about the tenuous and trembling threads of diplomacy. Hill insisted on having a detailed explanation of all the diplomatic policies of the Democratic administration.

" My dear young sir," said Mr. Adee, " this is a new administration, and I cannot see my way clear to discussing these matters with you as fully as you desire.

Mr. Adee is very deaf.

" If you can't tell me that," said Hill, in his ordinary tone of voice, " perhaps you can inform me whether or not it is true, as reported, that Noah built the ark."

When little Margaret passed her plate the third time for chicken her mother said:

" My dear, you must not eat so much chicken. I am afraid you'll be ill."

" Well, mother," said Margaret, " I'm not eating this because I want it. I'm collecting the bones for Fido ! "

Buck Bryant, the grandest and most redheaded fighter the State of North Carolina ever saw, has figured out to his own satisfaction who are the biggest fools in the world. He describes them as follows:

" The man who gets out in a boat and then rocks it for fun, the man who squints into a gun to see if it is loaded, and the man who goes for a ride on a bicycle and lets his baby sit on the handlebars."

They were on the subject of girls.

" Look here! " exclaimed McFarland. " Did you ever take a girl out to lunch when she felt a little faint? "

" Er — no," admitted Smith reluctantly.

" Well, take my advice and don't. One day I took Miss Jennie Westcott into a restaurant. At first she declined to eat anything, but then she said she believed she did feel a little faint."

" Did she take anything? "

" Did she take anything? She seized the menu, glanced over it, said she didn't feel very hungry and ordered " ——

" Well, what did she order? "

" Oysters, bouillon, lobster, cutlets, sweetbreads and peas, chicken, shrimp salad, biscuit glace, macaroons, coffee and creme de menthe. It cost me three dollars."

" Well, you ought to be glad," said Smith.

" Glad? What for? "

" Why, glad she wasn't hungry."

" Farmers take life a little easier, thanks to their various unions and combinations, than they used to do."

The speaker was John H. Kimble, of Port

Deposit, secretary of the Farmers' National Congress, an organization of three million farmers. He continued:

" Farmers are not nowadays like old Cornelius Husk. A new hand said to the old man one morning in the harvest season:

" ' I suppose you believe in the eight-hour system, Corney? '

" ' That's what I do,' grunted old Corn Husk, as he swung his pitchfork vigorously. ' Eight hours in the forenoon, eight hours in the afternoon and two or three hours overtime arter supper in the hay and harvest season — that's my system.' "

The pompous woman became acrimonious: " Do you call yourself a lady's maid? " she cried.

" I used to, ma'am," replied the servant, " before I worked for you."

" Do you think that Skinner can make a living out there in Australia? "

" Make a living! Why, he'd make a living on a rock in the middle of the ocean if there was another man on the rock."

Jim's boss sent him up on the roof to paint
it.   That was early in the morning.   Toward
nightfall the boss clambered up the ladder to
see whether his workman had flown away or
been eaten by the birds.   There was Jim sitting on the edge of the house, singing.

"Jim, you lazy piece, what you been doing?"

"Nuffin'."

"Didn't I send you up here to paint the
roof?"

"Yassir."

"Well, did you do it?"

"Yassir."

"What else did you do?"

"I went to sleep."

"Why didn't you come down if you had
finished?"

"'Deed, boss, you jes' said paint de roof.
You neveh said nuffin' 'bout comin' down."

Daniel G. Reid and Judge W. H. Moore,
the capitalists, are known in financial circles as
the Siamese twins of Wall Street.   They wan-
dered over to Jersey City one day to attend
an annual meeting of a corporation in which
both are heavily interested, and from which

both are said to have reaped millions. Returning to the ferryhouse on their way back, Mr. Reid strolled up to the ticket window and calmly said: "Two."

After going through all his pockets he turned to Moore. "Judge," he said, "you'll have to blow to the tickets. I'm broke."

"How much?" said the judge.

"Six cents," answered Reid.

"Gad," said Moore, "that's a life-saver. I've got just one dime."

Romance has many voices. It can be neither conjugated nor parsed.

The young man, who threw a duck fit every time he gazed upon the full and floating moon, was deeply attached to the girl who had a sense of humor.

"Ah!" sighed the youth, palpitating with those pulsations which indicate ardor. "I wish somebody would turn off the lights."

"Why?" inquired the girl, her face having a distinctly far-away look.

"Because, if they did," he sighed again, "I'd kiss you."

"Are you afraid," she asked, "to kiss me when they're turned on?"

The fellow who knew everybody of consequence in Washington wanted to get a six-
hundred-dollar job for an old-time friend.
This fellow who knew everybody was as full
of influence as a honeycomb is of honey. At
his request, senators, representatives, cabinet
members, State leaders, and even foreign am-
bassadors smote their arching heads with
their high silk hats and beat it rapidly to the
place where the influence was being concen-
trated like forty million sixteen-inch rapid-
firing guns.

The old-time friend did not get the job.

" By George! " said the fellow who knew
everybody. " Ain't that awful? We had as
much influence for him as if we'd been trying
to depose the pope! "

The red-headed and dissatisfied boarder
was a large man with a large appetite. After
dinner, he went out into the narrow yard,
shook both his fists at the silvery moon, hurled
several imprecations toward the congress of
the stars, and burst forth into a picturesque
and voluminous flood of abuse which was
devoted entirely to the landlady.

One of the other boarders, who had been

at the house a long time, thereby accumulating a pallid look and a palate with corns on it, drew near timidly and ventured to ask what the special kick was.

" What's the matter!" echoed the large man. " That old dame's the first woman I ever knew who could literally paint food on a plate."

Old Peterby is rich and stingy. In the event of his death his nephew will inherit his property. A friend of the family said to the old gentleman:

" I hear your nephew is going to marry. On that occasion you ought to do something to make him happy."

" I will," said Peterby; " I'll pretend that I am dangerously ill."

The father of a Denver bride presented his son-in-law with eighty thousand head of cattle.

" Papa, dear," exclaimed his daughter, fresh from an Eastern college, when she heard of it, " that was so kind of you. Charley's awfully fond of ox-tail soup."

Standing by the entrance of a large estate in the suburbs of Dublin are two huge dogs carved out of granite.

An Englishman going by in a motor thought he would have some fun with the Irish driver.

" How often, Mike, do they feed those two big dogs? "

" Whenever they bark, sir," was the straightforward reply.

It is said that the tragedies of early married life sometimes seem to lessen as they are seen through the perspective of years.

A young wife came to her mother-in-law with a heart-broken expression not long ago, and threw herself on the couch in the abandonment of grief.

" Why, Annette, what is the matter? " anxiously exclaimed the older woman. " Has anything happened to Frank? "

" Oh, mother, how can I tell you. He's taken to staying out nights! " cried the unhappy bride.

" How long has this been going on, dear? It doesn't seem possible! I used to know all about my boy's habits, and certainly that was

not among the number.   How late does he
stay away?"

"Well, you know he usually leaves the
office at five-thirty, mother.   Night before
last he never got home until twenty minutes
after six, and last night he never set foot in
the house until half-past six.   Oh, what shall
I do!"

MRS. W. (*at the matinée*): "Well, I de-
clare, there's actually somebody in the world
plainer than I am!   Look right over yonder
— But, no — see if you can find her."
MRS. Y. (*after searching diligently*): "I
can't find her."

Every mother knows of the time when
questions, often unanswerable, come too thick
and fast for the nerve-balance of a busy
housewife.
On baking-day mamma turned rather
crossly to little Elsie.
"For mercy's sake, stop asking so many
questions, child!"
"Well, mamma, just tell me this: which
is the front end of this biscuit?"

A group of grieving depositors stood on the sidewalk before the closed doors of a recently defunct bank. It wasn't a merry scene. One man who had lost his all was trying to brace up a colored grandpa whose white wool bobbed up and down into the folds of a bandana.

"Don't cry, Uncle," he said. "Banks burst every day, you know."

"Yes, sir, I know it, but — huh! huh! huh! — dis bank — huh! huh! — done bus' right in mah face!"

Years ago it used to be the custom of the country folk to work out their taxes by boarding the teacher, which meant that from time to time he was supplied from various quarters with food.

One day a boy named Elisha Anderson sought the teacher and said:

"Say, teacher, my pa wants to know if you like pork?"

"Indeed, I do," was the reply. "Say to your father that there is nothing in the way of meat I like better than pork."

Some time elapsed and there was no pork from Elisha's father, a fact that in no way surprised the teacher, for the old man was known throughout the country as a tight proposition. Nevertheless, one afternoon the teacher asked the boy:

" How about that pork, Elisha, that your father promised me? "

" Oh," answered the boy, " the pig got well."

Elizabeth and Amelia were chatting about a young man whom they both knew.

" I can't make anything of young Ralston, he's so stupid," said Elizabeth.

" Why, I don't think so," said Amelia. " He has a lot in him when you know him."

" Has he? " rejoined Elizabeth. " Well, then, I'm sure it's a vacant lot."

Mr. Jencks was visiting in the country, and near by lived a centenarian. One morning Mr. Jencks strolled over for a chat with the old man.

" To what do you attribute your longevity? " inquired the young man.

" To the fact," replied the old man, conclusively, " that I never died."

The celebrated French poet, Saint-Foix, who, in spite of his large income, was always in debt, sat one day in a barber's shop waiting to be shaved. He was lathered, when the door opened and a tradesman entered who happened to be one of the poet's largest creditors. No sooner did this man see Saint-Foix than he angrily demanded his money. The poet composedly begged him not to make a scene.

" Won't you wait for the money until I am shaved ? "

" Certainly," said the other, pleased at the prospect.

Saint-Foix then made the barber a witness of the agreement, and immediately took a towel, wiped the lather from his face, and left the shop. He wore a beard to the end of his days.

An old colored woman came into a Washington real-estate office the other day and was recognized as a tenant of a small house that had become much enhanced in value by reason of a new union station in that neighborhood.

" Look here, auntie, we are going to raise

your rent this month," the agent remarked briskly.

" 'Deed, an' Ah's glad to hear dat, sah," the old woman replied, ducking her head politely. " Mighty glad, fo' sho', case Ah des come in hyah ter-day ter tell yo' all dat Ah couldn't raise hit dis month."

Mrs. King was not accustomed to marketing, and knew nothing about it. One morning, shortly after the return from the wedding journey, she called at the market.

" You may send a nice piece of roast beef," she said to the butcher.

" Yes, ma'am," he replied.

" And," went on the young woman, with emphasis, " please have it very rare. My husband prefers it that way."

Mrs. Todd went into a store to buy some spring ginghams.

" Are these colors fast? " she asked the clerk.

" Yes, indeed," he replied earnestly; " you ought to see them when once they start to run."

Mrs. Marsden's only recommendation to society was the great wealth left her by an uncle.

"I attended the new theater last evening," she announced to a member of the smart set, whom she happened to meet one morning.

"Indeed!" said the social leader. "How are the acoustics of that theater?"

"The what?" queried Mrs. Marsden.

"The acoustic properties?" replied the other woman.

"Oh yes," said Mrs. Marsden, quickly — "the acoustic properties. Why, do you know, it struck me they were rather gaudy."

When little Philip and his mother took a trip to the mountains the car was so crowded that there were only two vacant seats, facing each other. She placed Philip on one seat and sat down opposite, saying, "Mamma will ride backward, as it does not make her sick."

Philip immediately began to cry, and the mother, much alarmed, asked if he were sick.

"No," sobbed Philip, "but I don't want you to go backward, mamma; I want to go to the same place that you go."

" Mr. Lane called again this morning, sir," said the new office-boy as Mr. Stuart entered the office.

" Did you tell him I'd gone to Europe, as I told you to, Edward? " asked Mr. Stuart.

" Yes, sir," answered the boy. " I told him you started this morning."

" That's a good boy," said Stuart. " And what did he say? "

" He wanted to know when you'd be back," replied Edward, " and I told him ' after lunch,' sir."

They must have long church services in a certain Western town where a paper announced of a certain church: " The regular services will commence next Sunday at 3 P. M., and continue until further notice."

" How does it happen," said the teacher to the new pupil, " that your name is Allen and your mother's name is Brown? "

" Well," explained the small boy, after a moment's thought, " you see, she married again and I didn't."

Robert had two little playfellows who were spending the afternoon with him. They finally began boasting about their parents and belongings.

" My father," bragged Robert, " is going to build a fine house with a steeple on it."

" That's nothing," exclaimed Louis, scornfully. " My father has just built a house with a flagpole on it."

Sherman, who had been listening intently, was silent for a moment, then burst forth, triumphantly:

" Gee, that's nothing. My father is going to build a corking house with a mortgage on it."

" This class comprehends the meaning of words very quickly," said the Boston teacher to her visitors. " You noticed we spoke of the word ' ransom ' a few minutes ago. How many " — turning to the children — " can think of a sentence containing the word ' ransom '? Every one. Yes, Harold? "

Harold arose proudly.

" My sister's beau ran some when Pa — "

And then the children wondered why the class was dismissed three minutes early.

Mr. Voelker was very fond of trout fishing, and each year tried to have at least a week of good sport. The day before he was to start on his long-looked-for vacation his wife, smiling joyously, entered the room, extending toward her husband some sticky, speckled papers.

" For goodness' sake, Laura," he exclaimed, " what on earth are you doing with those old fly-papers? "

" Why, I saved them for you from last summer, Jeff," she replied. " You know you said you always had to buy flies when you went fishing."

It was little Ruth's first time at a ball-game, and she was intensely interested in the different players. It was plainly seen, however, that the catcher, with his mask, breast-protector, and big mitt, was the hero in her admiring eyes.

" Which player do you like best, Ruth? " asked her father.

The expected answer, expressed in an unexpected way, came without hesitation:

" I like him best — that big man wif the dog face on."

Ann, aged four, accompanied her mother to the butcher shop. As she saw the sawdust-covered floor she exclaimed, " Oh, mamma, how many dolls this butcher has broken! "

He was always boasting about his ancestors and one day employed a genealogist to hunt them up. In due time the connoisseur of pedigrees returned and was cordially received by his patron.

" So you have succeeded in tracing back my ancestors? What is your fee? "

" Two hundred dollars. "

" Isn't that high? " objected the patron. " What's it for? "

" Principally, " responded the genealogist, " for keeping quiet about them. "

A banker was in the habit of wearing his hat a good deal during business hours, as in summer the flies used his bald pate for a parade ground, and in winter the cold breezes swept over its polished surface.

A negro workman on the railroad each week presented a check and drew his wages; and one day, as he put his money in a greasy wallet, the banker said: "Look here, Mose, why don't you let some of that money stay in the bank and keep an account with us?"

The negro leaned toward him, and, with a quizzical look at the derby the banker wore, answered confidentially:

"Boss, I's afeared. You look like you was always ready to start somewheres."

"Repeat the words the defendant used," said the lawyer for the plaintiff in a case of slander.

"I'd rather not," said the witness timidly; "they were hardly words to tell a gentleman."

"Ah," said the attorney, "then whisper them to the judge."

Little Tommy had spent his first day at school.

"What did you learn?" he was asked on his return home.

"Didn't learn nothin'."

"Well, what did you do?"

"Didn't do nothin'! A woman wanted to know how to spell 'cat,' and I told her."

The touring car had turned upside down, burying the motorist under it, but the village constable was not to be thus lightly turned from his duty.

"It's no use your hiding there," he said severely, "I must have your name and address."

"Fred Jenks is your next-door neighbor now, isn't he?" remarked a man while calling on a friend one evening.

"Who did you say?"

"Fred Jenks. I understand he is a finished cornetist."

"Is he? Good! Who did it?"

A certain young couple who were married some months ago never had a cloud to mar their happiness until recently. One morning the young wife came to breakfast in an extremely sullen and unhappy mood. To all her husband's inquiries she returned snappish answers. She was in no better frame of mind when he came home that evening for dinner, all of which mystified the young husband.

Finally, late in the evening, in reply to his

insistent demands to know what the matter was, the wife burst into tears and replied:

" Henry, if ever I dream again that you have kissed another woman I'll never speak to you as long as I live! "

" Well, well," said Dr. Bigbill, as he met a former patient on the street, " I'm glad to see you again, Mr. Brown. How are you this morning? "

" First, Doctor," said Mr. Brown cautiously, " does it cost anything to tell you? "

She was very stout and must have weighed nearly three hundred pounds. She was learning roller skating, when she had the misfortune to fall. Several attendants rushed to her side, but were unable to raise her at once. One said soothingly:

" We'll get you up all right, madam. Do not be alarmed."

" Oh, I'm not alarmed at all, but your floor is so terribly lumpy."

And then from underneath came a small voice which said: " I am not a lump, I am an attendant."

" Prosperity has ruined many a man," re-marked the moralizer.

" Well," rejoined the demoralizer, " if I was going to be ruined at all I'd prefer pros-perity to do it."

Sammy was not prone to overexertion in the classroom; therefore his mother was both surprised and delighted when he came home one noon with the announcement: " I got one hundred this morning."

" That's lovely, Sammy! " exclaimed his proud mother, and she kissed him tenderly. " What was it in? "

" Fifty in reading and fifty in 'rithmetic."

Once when John D. Rockefeller was play-ing golf a negro lad crossed the links. Mr. Rockefeller had just given the ball a vigorous stroke, and the lad received the missile squarely on the head. It was a heavy blow, but it only stunned the boy a little, and after blinking his eyes for a moment he was him-self again.

Mr. Rockefeller, who had rushed up fear-ing that the boy had been badly injured, was relieved to find that he took it so calmly, and, pulling a five-dollar bill from his pocket, he gave it to the youngster as a salve for his feelings.

The boy looked at the bill and grinned with delight. Then he looked at Mr. Rockefeller and inquired: " When is you goin' to be playin' again ? "

'A small boy had been vaccinated, and after the operation the doctor prepared to bandage the sore arm, but the boy objected.

" Put it on the other arm, Doctor."

" Why, no," said the physician, " I want to put the bandage on your sore arm, so the boys at school won't hit you on it."

" Put it on the other arm, Doc," reiterated the small boy; " you don't know the fellows at our school."

" Have you ever made a serious mistake in putting up a prescription ? " asked the customer of the apothecary.

" Never but once," said the drug man. " I charged a man thirty cents instead of a dollar and a half."

James started his third helping of pudding with delight.

" Once upon a time, James," admonished his mother, " there was a little boy who ate too much pudding, and he burst! "

James considered. " There ain't such a thing as too much pudding," he decided.

" There must be," contended his mother, " else why did the little boy burst? "

James passed his plate for the fourth time, saying: " Not enough boy."

" My son," said the father who was some-what addicted to moralizing, " this is the age of specialties and specialists. Is there anything you can do better than any one else in the world? "

" Yeth, thir," lisped the small boy; " I can read my own writing."

The lovely girl, having lingered a minute in her room to adjust her transformation, change the angle of her Grecian band and make sure that her skirt fitted like the peeling of a plum, descended to the parlor to find the family pet ensconced upon the knee of the young-man caller, her curly head nestled comfortably against his shoulder.

"Why, Mabel!" the young lady exclaimed; "aren't you ashamed of yourself? Get right down."

"Sha'n't do it," retorted the child. "I got here first."

"No," said the mistress of the boarding-house, "we cannot accommodate you, I am sorry to say. We only take in single gentlemen."

"Goodness!" said Mr. Borden; "what makes you think I'm twins?"

The oft-quoted Finnigan has a rival in Pat Donohue, an Ohio freight conductor whose train had a breakdown recently. After the accident he sent this message to Train Dispatcher Straight:

"Two-twenty-two has a busted flue. What will I do?   DONOHUE."

This awakened the slumbering muse in the telegraph office, and the reply ran:

"Wait. Two-twenty-eight will take your freight.   DISPATCHER STRAIGHT."

A man who kept a small shop was waiting on a single customer early one morning. His little boy and he were alone at the time, and the shopkeeper was obliged to go upstairs for some change. Before doing so he whispered to the little chap to watch the customer, to see that he didn't steal anything.

Very soon the proprietor returned with the necessary change, and the boy sang out: " He didn't steal anything, Pa; I watched him."

" Does the baby talk yet?" asked a friend of the family of the little brother.

" Naw," replied the little brother disgustedly. " He don't need to talk. All he has ter do is yell, and he gits everything in the house worth having."

Elihu Root tells a story about himself and his efforts to correct the manners of his office-boy. One morning the young autocrat came into the office, and, tossing his cap at a hook, exclaimed:

" Say, Mr. Root, there's a ball game down at the park to-day, and I want to go down."

Now the great lawyer was willing that the

boy should go, but thought he would teach him a little lesson in good manners.

"James," he said, "that isn't the way to ask a favor. Now you sit down in my chair and I'll show you how to do it properly."

The boy took the office chair, and his employer picked up his cap and stepped outside. He then opened the door softly, and, holding the cap in his hand, said quietly to the small boy in the big chair:

"Please, sir, there is a ball game at the park to-day; if you can spare me I would like to get away for the afternoon."

In a flash the boy responded:

"Why, certainly, Jimmie; and here is fifty cents to pay your way in."

Don't kick because you have to button your wife's waist. Be glad your wife has a waist, and doubly glad you have a wife to button a waist for. Some men's wives have no waists to button. Some men's wives' waists have no buttons on to button. Some men's wives' waists which have buttons on to button don't care a button whether they are buttoned or not. Some men don't have any wives with buttons on to button.

The aged lady next door had been quite ill, so one morning Willie's mother said to her small son:

"Willie, run over and see how old Mrs. Smith is this morning."

Willie departed, but in a few moments he came running back and said:

"She says it's none of your business."

"Why, Willie!" exclaimed his mother. "What did you ask her?"

"Just what you told me to," said Willie; "I said you wanted to know how old she was."

"After I wash my face I look in the mirror to see if it's clean. Don't you?" asked the sweet little girl of Bobbie.

"Don't have to," said Bobbie; "I just look at the towel."

"Why don't you run for office?"

"I've thought about it," replied Mr. Dustin Stax; "but I'm satisfied to subscribe to campaign funds. The fact that a man is willing to give prizes for airship flights doesn't put him under obligations to aviate."

They had just become engaged.

"Oh, Will," she said, moving a trifle closer to him, "I am so glad you are not rich! They say that some of those millionaires receive threatening letters saying that something dreadful will happen to them if they don't pay the writers sums of money."

"Oh, is that all?" replied Will. "Why, I get plenty of such letters."

Two young bootblacks who have stands close together on Tremont Street quarreled the other day. "I'll get even with that guy yet," vowed the smaller boy of the two.

"Goin' to fight him, are yer, Jimmy?" he was asked.

"Naw! When he gets troo polishin' a gent I'm goin' to say ter that gent soon's he steps off the chair: 'Shine, sir, shine!'"

"Where is Henry?" asked the neighbor of the lady whose husband he wanted to see.

"I don't know exactly," said the wife; "if the ice is as thick as Henry thinks it is he is skating; if it is as thin as I think it is he is swimming."

The following story of an English noble-man, now deceased, was recently told in a London club.

" The duke was once in church when a collection was announced for some charitable object. The plate began to go round, and the duke carefully put his hand into his pocket and took out a florin, which he laid on the pew before him ready to be transferred to the plate.

" Beside him sat a little snob, who, noticing this action, imitated it by ostentatiously laying a sovereign alongside the ducal florin. This was too much for his grace, who dipped his hand into his pocket again and pulled out another florin, which he laid by the side of the first. The little snob followed suit by laying another sovereign beside the first. His grace quietly added a third florin, which was capped by a third sovereign on the part of the little snob. Out came a fourth florin to swell the duke's donation, and then the little snob triumphantly laid three sovereigns at once upon the board. The duke, not to be beaten, produced three florins.

" Just at this moment the plate arrived. The little snob took up his handful of sovereigns, ostentatiously rattled them into the plate, then turned defiantly toward his rival, as if he would say, ' I think that takes the rise out of you.'

" Fancy his chagrin when the duke, with a grim smile, put one florin into the plate, and quietly swept the remaining six back into his pocket ! "

" Do moind yez don't git hur-rt, Pat," said Bridget, as her liege lord started to work. " It's so dangerous a-workin' in that quarry."

" Thot's ahl roight, Biddy," said Pat. " Oi've borryed two dollars frim th' foreman, and he don't let me do any dangerous work anny more."

A medical student was talking to a surgeon about a case.

" What did you operate on the man for? " the student asked.

" Three hundred dollars," replied the surgeon.

" Yes, I know," said the student. " I mean, what did the man have? "

" Three hundred dollars," replied the surgeon.

The honest farmer who took in summer boarders greeted the new arrivals with truly rural enthusiasm.

" I swan, I'm right deown glad to meet ye," he cried as he extended his horny hand. " Heow's th' folks to hum? "

The man of the party looked at the enthusiast with some suspicion.

" Farmer," he said, " your dialect strongly reminds me of the stage variety."

The agriculturist grinned.

" It's all right, ain't it? " he asked. " I gave an actor feller a month's board free to teach it to me."

" I have invented a new dance."

" What do you call it? "

" ' The Wall Street Wallop.' You swing corners, change partners, and side-step."

" Thirty cents a word for this stuff? " exclaimed the editor. " I wouldn't think of it."

" Sir, I am a famous author."

" That's just it. You are a famous author, not a famous pugilist or a successful spitball pitcher."

Mr. Cooke was a traveling man, and was slightly injured in a railroad accident. One of the officials of the road went to his home to break the news gently to Mrs. Cooke.

"Madam," he began, "be calm! Your husband has met with a slight — that is to say, one of the drive-wheels of a passenger locomotive struck him on the cheek, and — "

"Well, sir," interrupted the woman, "you needn't come around here trying to collect any damages of me. You won't get a cent! If your company can't keep its property out of danger, it'll have to take the consequences. You should have your engines insured."

"I suppose you are mama's darling?"

"No, ma'am, I am my mama's moving picture."

"Your mama's moving picture?"

"Yessum, she is always telling me that I should be seen and not heard."

"I called a doctor last night."

"Was anybody sick?"

"Yes; he was when he saw the hand I held."

The scene is set.

A country road, trees, sky, summer homes, a lake in the distance. A steam-railway line crosses the road at right angles.

Enter, up the road, an automobile, well loaded and running at high speed.

Enter at the far right an express train.

Both automobile and train are rushing toward the crossing.

Owner of automobile to chauffeur: "Can you make it?"

The chauffeur speeding up: "Sure I can make it!"

He doesn't.

"If there were four flies on a table and I killed one, how many would be left?" inquired the teacher.

"One," answered a bright little girl — "the dead one."

"No man can serve two masters," observed the good parson who was visiting the penitentiary.

"I know it," replied Convict 1313. "I'm in here for bigamy."

Louis J. Horowitz, the sky-scraper builder, who in twenty years has risen from a position of $3 a week to one of $100,000 a year, was talking about success.

"I go to bed at 9 o'clock," he said, "and I get up at 5 o'clock. I play a little, but my play is exercise to keep me in good trim for my office. I play to work — as other men work to play."

Mr. Horowitz mused a moment; then in his terse, epigrammatic way he said, shaking his head:

"Success demands sacrifice! Two men set out to achieve fame. One succeeded. The other lived."

The judge of a Texas county was also cashier of the town bank. One day a stranger presented a check for payment and his evidence of identification was not satisfactory.

"Why, Judge," said the man, "I've known you to sentence men to prison for life on no better evidence than this!"

"That may be true," replied the Judge. "But when it comes to handing out cold cash we have to be mighty careful."

"I understand that you have a fine track team here," said the visitor to the guide who was showing him through the college. "What individual holds most of the medals?"

The guide pondered. "Well, sir," he said, "I guess it is the pawnbroker down town."

"Now, Harold," said the teacher, "if there were eleven sheep in a field and six jumped the fence, how many would there be left?"

"None," replied Harold.

"Why, yes, there would."

"No," he persisted; "you may know arithmetic, but you don't know sheep."

A man was fixing his automobile.

"Trouble?" asked a bystander.

"Some," was the laconic answer.

"What power car is it?"

"Forty-horse," came the answer.

"What seems to be the matter with it?"

"Well, from the way she acts I should say that thirty-nine of the horses were dead."

John, a rather backward rustic, sat at one end of the sofa and his sweetheart at the other. Both minds were too full to carry on conversation, but at last the lady spoke:

"John, what are you thinking about?"

John, awakened from his dreams, answered with a drawl, "Oh, jest the same as you are," and was surprised to get the retort:

"If you do I'll slap you."

"Did the doctor tell you what you had?"

"No. He took what I had without telling me."

Going to the blackboard the teacher wrote this sentence: "The horse and the cow was in the stable."

"Now, children," she said, "there is something wrong with that sentence. Who can correct it and tell why it is wrong?"

One small boy waved his hand excitedly and the teacher called upon him.

"It's wrong," he said with importance. "It should be the cow and the horse was in the stable, because ladies always ought to go first."

A heavy bunch of clouds passed over Hog-wallow yesterday bound for a Sunday-school picnic in progess near Rye Straw.

On moving into a new neighborhood the small boy of the family was cautioned not to fight with his new acquaintances. One day Tommy came home with a black eye and badly bespattered with mud.

"Why, Tommy," said his mother, " didn't I tell you not to fight until you had counted one hundred?"

"Yes'm," sniffled Tommy; " and look what Willie Smith did while I was counting."

" I've figured the whole thing out, Father," said Mabel. " The car, to begin with, will cost five thousand dollars, which at six per cent. is three hundred dollars a year. If we charge ten per cent. off for depreciation it will come to five hundred dollars more. A good chauffeur can be had for one hundred and twenty-five dollars a month, or fifteen hundred dollars a year. I have allowed ten dollars a week for gasoline and five dollars for repairs. The chauffeur's uniform and furs will come to about two hundred dollars. Now let's see what it comes to: Three hundred plus five hundred —— "

" Don't bother, my dear, I know what it comes to," said the old gentleman.

" What? " asked the girl.

" My dear," said the father impressively, " it comes to a standstill, right here and now."

A certain careless student in a small college suffered from obesity, and it appears that even college professors do not love a fat man. One day, after a particularly unsuccessful recitation in mathematics, the instructor said scornfully: " Well, Mr. Blank, you are better fed than taught."

" That's right, Professor," sighed the youth, subsiding heavily into his chair; " you teach me — I feed myself."

" Did you kill the moths with the moth balls I recommended? " asked the druggist.

" No I didn't! " said the customer truculently; " I sat up all night and didn't hit a single moth."

Dick heard of Lou's engagement and went around to congratulate him.

"Well, old boy," cried Dick, as he grasped his friend's hand, "my congratulations! Is it true that you are engaged to one of the pretty Robbins twins?"

"Yes," replied Lou heartily, "I am happy to say it is so."

"But," inquired Dick, "how do you ever tell them apart?"

"I don't try to," was the reply.

A judge in a Western town had declared that he would stop the carrying of firearms on the street. Before him appeared for trial a tough youth charged with getting drunk and firing his revolver in a crowded street.

"Twenty dollars and costs," said the magistrate.

"But, your honor," interposed counsel for the prisoner, "my client did not hit anybody."

"Why, you admit that he fired the gun?"

"Yes, but he fired it into the air," explained the lawyer.

"Twenty dollars and costs," repeated the judge. "He might have shot an angel."

The little son of the physician, together with a friend, was playing in his father's office during the absence of the doctor, when suddenly the young host threw open a closet door and disclosed to the terrified gaze of his little friend an articulated skeleton.

When the visitor had sufficiently recovered from his shock to stand the announcement the doctor's son explained that his father was extremely proud of that skeleton.

" Is he? " asked the other. " Why? "

" I don't know," was the answer; " maybe it was his first patient."

The maiden lady of uncertain age became very indignant when the census taker asked her age.

" Did you see the girls next door? " she asked; " the Hill twins? "

" Certainly," replied the census man.

" And did they tell you their age? "

" Yes."

" Well," she snapped as she shut the door in his face, " I'm just as old as they are! "

" Oh, very well," said the census man to himself, and he wrote down in his book:

" Jane Johnson — as old as the Hills."

"That large bump running across the back of your head," said the phrenologist, "means that you are inclined to be curious, even to the point of recklessness."

"I know it," said the man who was consulting him; "I got that bump by sticking my head into the dumb-waiter shaft to see if the waiter was going up, and it was coming down."

A little boy had been punished by his mother one day, and that night at bedtime he prayed thus:

"Dear Lord, bless Papa and Sister Lucy and Brother Frank and Uncle Fred and Aunt Mary and make me a good boy. Amen."

Then looking up into his mother's face he said: "I suppose you noticed that you weren't in it."

"Yes," said the severe maiden lady, "the word 'mule' is only 'male' spelled wrongly."

"I suppose so," responded the crusty bachelor; "but according to the Latin dictionary a woman is 'mulier.'"

" Did you come out well on Christmas, Willie?" asked the Sunday-school teacher.

" Yes'm. I got more than any of my brothers and sisters," replied Willie jubilantly.

" Indeed? How did that happen?"

" I got up two hours before they did."

It happened the other evening, and now a certain clubman is trying to figure out how he will square things with his wife the next time he is " detained " down town. He was not going home for dinner, and when his wife answered the telephone he said: " Don't wait for me at dinner this evening, dear. I shall be detained on business."

" Very well," she replied. " I'm sorry you can't come home; but business is business, I suppose. Where are you now?"

" Where am I? In my office of course. I have had a very busy day."

" It's too bad you have to work so hard, George. But tell me something."

" Yes, dear. What is it?"

" How can you keep your mind on business with the orchestra playing 'Every Little Movement?' "

If wisdom's ways you wisely seek,
    Five things observe with care:
Of whom you speak, to whom you speak,
    And how, and when, and where.

Two men were discussing the friends of their boyhood and mentioned one who had a most unfortunate disposition.

" I wonder what became of him," said one of the men. " It always seemed to me that it would be impossible for him to find any work that would be congenial."

" I thought so too," said his friend, " but we were wrong. He's got a job that suits him perfectly. He's station master in a place where there are eighty trains a day and he sees somebody miss every one of them."

A company promoter advertised for an office boy. He received a hundred replies. Out of the hundred he selected ten, and with the writers of these ten replies he had a personal interview. His final choice fell upon a bright youth, to whom he said: " My boy, I like your appearance and your manner very much. I think you may do for the place.

Did you bring a character?" "No, Sir," replied the boy; "I can go home and get it." "Very well; come back to-morrow morning with it, and if it is satisfactory I daresay I shall engage you." Late that afternoon the financier was surprised by the return of the candidate. "Well," he said cheerily, "have you got your character?" "No," answered the boy; "but I've got yours — an' I ain't coming!"

An automobilist who was touring through the country saw, walking ahead of him, a way-worn man, followed by a mangy dog. As the machine drew near them the dog started suddenly to cross the road. He was hit by the car and killed. The motorist stopped his machine and approached the man.

"I'm very sorry, my man, that this has happened," he said. "Will $10.00 settle it?"

"Oh! yes," said the man, "$10.00 will suffice."

Pocketing the money as the car disappeared in the distance, he looked down at the dead animal. "I wonder whose dog it was?" he said.

A minister in a small Western town surprised his audience one Sunday by reading the following notice from the pulpit:

" The regular session of the Donkey Club will be held as usual after the service. Members will line up just outside the door, make remarks and stare at the ladies who pass, as is their custom."

The club didn't meet that Sunday.

" Before we were married, Henry," said the young wife reproachfully, " you always gave me the most beautiful Christmas presents. Do you remember? "

" Sure," said Henry cheerfully; " but, my dear, did you ever hear of a fisherman giving bait to a fish after he had caught it? "

A young lady telephone operator recently attended a watch-night service and fell asleep during the sermon. At the close the preacher said: " We will now sing hymn number three forty-one — three forty-one."

The young lady, just waking in time to hear the number, yawned and said: " The line is busy. Please call again."

" The train struck the man, did it not? " asked the lawyer of the engineer at the trial.

" It did, sir," said the engineer.

" Was the man on the track, sir? " thundered the lawyer.

" On the track? " asked the engineer. " Of course he was. No engineer worthy of his job would run his train into the woods after a man, sir."

" Willie," admonished the mother, " why don't you let your little brother have your sled some of the time? "

" Why, I do, Mamma," said Willie. " He has it half the time. I take it going down hill and he has it coming back."

A teacher recently received the following from the mother of an absent pupil:

Dere mam: please eggscuse Willy. He didn't have but one pair of pants an' I kep him home to wash them and Mrs. O'Toole's goat come and et them off the line and that awt to be eggscuse enuff, goodness nose.

Yours with respeck,
Mrs. B.

" Little pictures leave me cold; it's the grand big canvases that I like."

" You're an art critic? "

" Not I; a frame maker."

" I am glad to see you home, Johnny," said the father to his small son who had been away at school, but who was now home on his Christmas vacation. " How are you getting on at school? "

" Fine," said Johnny. " I have learned to say ' Thank you ' and ' If you please ' in French."

" Good! " said the father. " That's more than you ever learned to say in English."

A section foreman on a railroad was ordering a list of supplies. He had completed his letter when he found he was in need of a " frog " for a switch, so his letter ran as follows:

MR. SUPERVISOR.

Dear Sir: You will please ship me some pick handles, spike mauls, spikes and wrenches.   Yours truly,

PAT HOGAN and a frog.

The young lady who wished to buy some mistletoe was astonished at the high price, and protested to the clerk.

"Well," said the wise salesman, "if you want it for decoration it comes high, but if you want it for business any old twig will do just as well."

Two actors were boasting about their dramatic exploits.

"Aha, my boy!" said one, "when I played 'Hamlet' the audience took fifteen minutes to leave the theatre."

The other looked at him.

"Was he lame?" he inquired gently.

Old Mr. Anderson, who was fond of relating stories of the war, after the Christmas dinner was over mentioned having been in five engagements.

"That's not so much," said little Edgar suddenly.

"Why, Edgar!" cried his scandalized mother; "what do you mean?"

"Five isn't many," persisted Edgar; "sister Edna has been engaged nine times."

" Sure," said Pat, on Christmas morning, rubbing his hands at the prospect of a present, " Oi always done me duty an' Oi always mane to do it."

" I believe you, Pat," said his employer, who was the head of a big trust, " and therefore I shall make you a present of all you have stolen from me during the year."

" Thank your Honor," said Pat, " an' may all yer business acquaintances treat you as liberally."

" Well, my little man, what can I do for you ? " asked the grocer, as he rubbed his hands genially together.

" Please, sir, mother says these matches she bought this morning ain't no good."

" No good ! " exclaimed the grocer, now looking almost as much worried as the boy. " What's the matter with them ? This is the first complaint I've had."

" Can't help that," said the small boy; " mother says they ain't no good."

" Nonsense ! " replied the grocer. Then, taking a match from one of the boxes, he gave it a smart rub, which ignited it immediately, and turned to the boy again.

" Well," he inquired, " what have you got to say now? "

The small complainant returned the disdainful look, undaunted.

" That's orl right, guv'nor," he remarked; " but d'you fink my muvver's coming 'ere to strike matches on your boot every time she wants a light? "

A prominent Chicago politician, when a candidate for an important municipal office, related the following story of his campaign.

" Once I told three negroes that I'd give a big turkey to the one who'd give the best reason for his being a Republican.

" The first one said: ' I'se a 'publican kase de 'publican set us niggers free.'

" ' Very good, Pete,' said I. ' Now, Bill, let me hear from you.'

" ' Well, I'se a 'publican kase dey don' gib us a pertective tariff.'

" ' Fine! ' I exclaimed. ' Now, Sam, what have you to say? '

" ' Boss,' said Sam, scratching his head and shifting from one foot to the other, ' boss, I'se a 'publican kase I wants dat turkey.'

" And he got it."

A man left his umbrella in a stand at a hotel recently, with a card attached bearing this inscription: —

" This umbrella belongs to a man who can deal a blow of 250 pounds weight. I shall be back in five minutes."

When he returned to claim his property, he found in its place a card bearing the following inscription: —

" This card was left here by a man who can run twelve miles an hour. I shall not come back."

The late Major Barttelot was educated at Rugby, where he is still remembered as the hero of one of the most delightful of school-boy blunders. " What is the meaning of the word ' adage ' ? " was the question asked by the master. It came to young Barttelot, who, without hesitation, replied, " A place to put cats into."   Every one laughed; and the master, as much mystified as the rest, called him up at the end of the lesson, and asked him what had put such an idea into his head. " Well, sir," said Barttelot, looking injured, " doesn't it say in Shakespere, ' Like the poor cat in the adage ' ? "

The newly married couple had gone West to live, and as the Christmas season drew nigh she became homesick.

" Even the owls are different here," she sighed.

" And how is that? " he asked.

" Here they say ' To-hoot-to-who,' and in Boston they say ' To-hoot-to-whom.' "

Anna Dickenson was lecturing some years ago in Chicago. In her lecture she paused and queried, " Oh, why was I born? "

Some one called out in the gallery, " It can't be helped now; go on."

A college student handed in a paper to his professor, and was surprised the next day to have it returned with a note scrawled on the margin. He studied it diligently, but was unable to decipher the note, and so he brought his paper back to the professor. " I can't quite make out what this is, if you please," said the student. " That, sir? " said the professor. " Why, that says, ' I cannot read your handwriting.' You write illegibly, sir, a very bad practice."

"You know, Dorothy, these biscuits of yours," he began, as he helped himself to the seventh. "Yes?" said his wife, with a weary smile. "Ah! they're nothing like mother's." "No?" The smile was gone. "No. Not a bit. You see, mother's were heavy and gave me dyspepsia, while yours are as light as a feather, and I can eat about — why, what's the matter, Dorothy?" She had fainted.

The semi-weekly conferences at the White House which President Wilson has held with the newspaper correspondents have afforded opportunity to exhibit the many very human traits which he possesses. They have produced many a good story, too, for the President is very fond of illustrating a point he wishes to make by telling a yarn.

For instance, quite recently he was closely catechised by the correspondents as to his position on the question as to whether or not there were items in the Underwood Tariff bill which might be the subject of compromise. This brought the following Lincoln story:

"Mr. Lincoln once told this story," said

the President. "He had spent a whole evening with a gentleman whom he was sending on a confidential mission and when the evening was over the gentleman said: 'Well, Mr. President, is there anything we have overlooked? Have you any general instructions that you can give me?' and Mr. Lincoln said: 'I will say what my little neighbor in Springfield said. On her sixth birthday she had received some alphabet blocks with which she was very much charmed and was allowed to take them to bed with her, great to her delight.

"'She played with them until she got so sleepy that she could hardly see the blocks. She remembered that she had not said her prayers and so she got on her knees again and said: "Oh, Lord, I am too sleepy to pray; there are the blocks; spell it out for yourself."'"

At the same interview the correspondents were very anxious to know if the President was in favor of public hearings on the Tariff bill. This is what Mr. Wilson said:

"You know what Artemus Ward said. He said: 'When I see a snake hole I walk around it; because I say to myself, "That is a snake hole."'"

Little Tommy had just been promoted from the Kindergarten to the First Form, where the boys were doing history.

"Now," said the master, "Queen Mary followed King Edward VI. Can any of you tell me who followed Mary?"

Tommy saw a chance to distinguish himself.

"I know," he cried triumphantly. "Her little lamb!"

William had just returned from college, resplendent in peg-top trousers, silk hosiery, a fancy waistcoat and a necktie that spoke for itself. He entered the library where his father was reading. The old gentleman looked up and surveyed his son. The longer he looked the more disgusted he became.

"Son," he finally blurted out, "you look like a d— fool!"

Later the old major who lived next door came in and greeted the boy heartily. "William," he said, with undisguised admiration, "you look exactly like your father did twenty years ago when he came back from school!"

"Yes," replied William, with a smile, "so father was just telling me."

Captain Rostron of the *Carpathia,* while attending a dinner recently in New York was talking on the subject of ability. " The ability to state a case so clearly as to render misunderstanding impossible, is a natural gift," the Captain remarked. " But, unfortunately, all persons do not possess it. A political convention was being held for the purpose of nominating a candidate for an important office.

" The district was a close one, and the necessity of selecting a popular man was thoroughly recognized. A speaker had just nominated a personal friend for the position, and in an elaborate eulogy had presented in vivid terms his manifold merits, especially emphasizing his great services upon the field of battle, as well as in the pursuits of peace.

" As the speaker resumed his seat a voice from the rear of the room rang out: ' Well, what we want is a man that will run the best.'

" Instantly the alert orator was on his feet again.

" ' If you think this convention can find anybody who can run better than the gentleman I have nominated, I point you once more to his well-known war record,' the speaker shouted with a wave of his hand."

Little Molly sat down to write a letter to her father, who had been absent three months, and this is what she finally sent:

" DEAR FATHER:— We are all well and happy. The baby has grown ever so much and has a great deal more sense than he used to have. Hoping the same of you, I remain your daughter, Molly."

This advertisement recently appeared in a Western paper:

" WANTED — A man to undertake the sale of a new patent medicine. The advertiser guarantees that it will be profitable to the undertaker."

One of the best-known astronomers was talking about the difficulties and intricacies that astronomy presents to the popular mind.

" For instance," he said, smiling, " there is the story of the meteorite that fell on an Essex farm a year ago. It was a valuable meteorite, and the landlord claimed it at once.

" ' All minerals and metals on the land belong to me,' he said. ' That's in the lease.'

" But the tenant demurred. ' This meteorite,' he said, ' wasn't on the farm, you must remember, when the lease was drawn up.'

" This was certainly a poser, but the land-lord was equal to the occasion, for he promptly retorted: ' Well, then, I claim it as flying game.'

" But the tenant was ready for him. ' It's got neither wings nor feathers,' he said. ' Therefore as ground game it is mine.'

" How long they would have continued their argument I cannot say, for at that moment a revenue officer came up and proceeded to take possession of the meteorite. ' Because,' said he, ' it is an article introduced into this country without payment of duty.' "

It was Casey's first ocean trip. The doctor found him doubled up in his berth suffering from sea-sickness; and, wishing to cheer him up said: " I know you are in great pain, Casey, but brace up and act like the man I take you for; it will soon be over; you're not going to die."

" Oi ain't going to die! " exclaimed Casey. " Phaix, doctor, Oi thought Oi would, and that was the only thing that was keeping me alive."

The geography class was in session, and the teacher pointed a finger to the map on the class-room wall.

" Here, on one hand, we have the far-stretching country of Russia. Willie," she asked, looking over her pupils and settling on one small boy at the end of the class," what do you see on the other hand? "

Willie, hopeless with fright, hesitated a moment, and then answered: " Warts! "

One day two lawyers who were pleading a case became angry and one of them said:

" That attorney is the ugliest and meanest lawyer in the county."

" You forget yourself, you forget yourself, Mr. Smith," said the court, rapping with his gavel.

Of all the witty things said or written by Mark Twain, no phrase has been quoted oftener than his reply to an alarmist report, " Rumor of my death greatly exaggerated." The history of this now celebrated *bon mot* will doubtless be of interest. Mark Twain was on a visit to London some years ago, and had been secured as the chief guest at a dinner to be given by a literary club. On the morning of the day when the dinner was to take place the secretary was shocked to hear a rumor that Mark Twain had died suddenly. At his wit's end, he sought to verify it by a diplomatic note to Mrs. Clemens, in which he mentioned the rumor. Mark Twain got hold of the note and telegraphed the now-famous reply, " Rumor of my death greatly exaggerated."

" Ah," sighed the boarder who was given to rhapsodies, as they sat down to the Christmas dinner, " if we could only have one of those turkeys that we used to raise on the farm when I was a boy!"

" Oh, well," said the pessimistic boarder, " perhaps it is one. You never can tell."

" You eat very little, Mr. Smith," said the maiden coyly to the bashful lover who had been invited to share the family Christmas dinner.

" Yes," replied he, and for once he saw a chance and, grasping his courage, he said: " To sit next to you, Miss Grace, is to lose one's appetite."

" What's the shape of the earth? " asked the teacher, calling suddenly upon Willie.

" Round."

" How do you know it's round? "

" All right," said Willie; " it's square then. I don't want to start any argument about it."

Louise had made loud and repeated calls for more turkey at the Christmas dinner. After she had disposed of a liberal quantity she was told that too much turkey would make her sick. Looking wistfully at the fowl for a moment she said:

" Well, give me anuzzer piece an' send for the doctor."

There is as much philosophy as fun in the Irishman's reply, printed below, which, of course, does not detract from the humor of it.

A man was seen, one hot summer day, laboriously turning a windlass which hoisted a bucket of rock from the shaft. There was nothing remarkable about the man except his hat, the crown of which had been cut in such a manner that the hot sun beat upon his bald head continually. Some of his companions had recommended this as sure to produce a luxuriant head of hair.

After watching the man toiling and grunting at his heavy labor for a while, a lawyer who was passing said with concern,

" My friend, why don't you cover up your head? This hot sun will affect your brain."

" Brain, is it? " said the man, as he gave the windlass another turn. " Be jabers, and if I had any brains d'ye think I'd be here pullin' up this bucket? "

A certain gentleman high up in the political world delivered an address before the Greek class of a large university about which a reporter wrote as follows:

" Mr. Blank spoke to the class in the purest ancient Greek, without mispronouncing a word or making the slightest grammatical solecism."

" How did the reporter know that? " remarked one senator to another on reading the account in the paper.

" I told him," was the answer.

" But you don't know Greek."

" True; but I know a little about politics."

Mrs. Black woke her husband one night and whispered: "Larry, there's a burglar in the parlor! He just bumped against the piano and struck several keys."

"Is that so?" said Larry. "I'll go right down there."

"Oh, Larry," whispered the excited wife, "don't do anything rash!"

"Rash!" replied the husband. "Why, I'm going to help him. You don't suppose he can move that piano from the house without assistance, do you?"

A Southern congressman, who formerly practised law in Mississippi, tells of an amusing case he once tried in that state. He was then a student in the office of his uncle, a Col. Martin who figured in local politics.

The main figure in the trial was a lazy darky named Dick Sutton, arrested at the instance of his wife, who alleged that he contributed nothing to her support and refused to work.

During the examination of Sutton the young lawyer asked:

"Dick, have you any fixed income?"

Sutton was puzzled by the term. Counsel

explained that the expression meant a certainty of money paid not for odd jobs but for steady employment; in other words, a compensation at stated intervals on which one could absolutely rely.

Upon the conclusion of counsel's remarks the darky's face brightened.

"I think I have a fixed income, sah," said he.

"And what is this fixed income?" was the next question.

"Well, sah," answered Dick with a broad grin in the direction of Col. Martin, "de colonel dere allers gives me fo' dollars and a sack o' flour on 'lection day!"

If a Hottentot taught a Hottentot tot
    To talk ere the tot could totter,
Ought the Hottentot tot
To be taught to say "aught"
    Or "naught," or what ought to be taught
        her?

If to hoot and toot a Hottentot tot
    Be taught by a Hottentot tooter,
Should the tooter get hot if the Hottentot tot
    Hoot and toot at the Hottentot tutor?

Before the guests had arrived for the Christmas party the girls had congregated in the lower hall, conversing on topics nearest their hearts.

"Oh, girls!" said Dolly; "I know a new charm to tell when one loves you."

"What is it?" queried the chorus.

"You take five or six chestnuts, name each after some man you know, and then put them on the stove. The first one that pops is the one that loves you."

"H'm," said the beautiful young blonde, toying with a new diamond ring; "I know a much better way than that."

"What?"

"Select one man, place him on a sofa in the parlor and sit close to him, with a dim light. If he doesn't pop it's time to change the man on the sofa."

(9)